the ANTI 9 to 5 GUIDE

practical CAREER advice for WOMEN who think outside the CUBE

Michelle Goodman

D0711295

SEAL PRESS

THE ANTI 9-TO-5 GUIDE

Practical Career Advice for Women Who Think Outside the Cube

Copyright © 2007 by Michelle Goodman

Published by
Seal Press
1400 65th Street, Suite 250
Emeryville, CA 94608

Library of Congress Cataloging-in-Publication Data

Goodman, Michelle, 1967-
The anti 9-to-5 guide : practical career advice for women who think outside the cube / Michelle Goodman.
        p. cm.
Includes bibliographical references.
ISBN-13: 978-1-58005-186-6 (alk. paper)
ISBN-10: 1-58005-186-3 (alk. paper)
1. Vocational guidance for women. 2. Women—Employment—Psychological aspects.
3. Quality of work life. 4. Self-actualization (Psychology). 5. Career development.
I. Title. II. Title: Career advice for women who think outside the cube.

HF5382.6.G66 2007
650.1082—dc22
2006030695

9 8 7 6 5 4 3

Cover & interior design by Kate Basart/Union Pageworks
Printed in the United States of America by Berryville

To my mom, the first career woman in my life.

And to Grandpa Jack, the first entrepreneur who inspired me.

"I'm not gonna spend the rest of my life working my ass off and getting nowhere just because I followed rules that I had nothing to do with setting up."

—Melanie Griffith as Tess McGill in *Working Girl,* 1988

CONTENTS

Introduction,

or how I fled

the CUBE

Back when I was a wage slave, sleep didn't come easy. Sometimes I'd spend the wee morning hours fixated on my bedroom ceiling, stressing about the three days' worth of work some joker had assigned me at five o'clock that afternoon—inevitably accompanied by sticky notes covered with red exclamation points, and an impossible deadline just twenty-four hours away. Or my sleep would be riddled with those ever-dreaded work dreams. There I'd be in my flannel jammies, slumbering far from peacefully as my dreams transported me to my grim gray cubicle. And there Dreamstate Me would be seated at my workstation, editing the same technical documentation Wakingstate Me would have to edit the next day when I actually got out of bed and dragged my bleary-eyed self into the office. Not only was I cheating myself out of a good night's sleep, I was doing the same onerous job one time too many.

Perhaps I just needed to learn to relax, take up Xanax, desk yoga, or transcendental commuter meditation. But I like to think I'm just not hardwired for office work and all the groveling, commuting, and Monday morning staff meetings that come with it. To me, the devil doesn't wear Prada—the devil wears pantyhose.

That's why, in my mid-twenties, after one fitful night too many, I got myself a pair of bunny slippers and began dabbling in all things anti 9-to-5: freelancing, temping, telecommuting, part-time work, flextime work, self-employment, you name it. As long as the work was somewhat related to writing and didn't involve sitting at someone else's desk a full forty hours a week, I was game. (Okay, maybe typing up the erotic Wiccan poetry manuscripts of art students wasn't *writing*, per se, but it seemed like a close cousin at the time. Plus, it meant I could work from home.)

As a cubicle expat, I still couldn't sleep, but it was because I was so amped about landing an editing project with an honest-to-goodness publisher (of calculus textbooks!) or a couple of 300-word writing assignments for some obscure, artsy newsletter with a whopping circulation of eleven. Piddly assignments soon became stepping-stones to beefier ones, though, and within a few years, I graduated to writing and editing for household-name companies and publications, effectively quelling all inquiries from family about when I was going to get a "real job."

When I started working for myself back in the Middle Ages, I didn't have a mentor, a guidebook, a Rolodex, or any freelance friends to talk shop with. Web surfing was a relatively new phenomenon (Google and Blogger had yet to debut), so I didn't have today's wealth of information at my fingertips. I also didn't have a clue, seeing as I left the cushy world of biweekly paychecks without so much as reading a book on self-employment, let alone securing a solid client base or saving up a couple hundred bucks. (Lesson learned: Leaping before you look is stupid.) Consequently, I discovered how to work outside the cube "on the job"—and by screwing up a whole lot of things, from my first few freelance projects (for ye olde college textbook publisher) to my credit rating.

By the time I finally got around to perusing the self-employment shelf at the bookstore several years later, I felt like an imposter, like I didn't belong in the DIY-career club. Where were the career manuals for creative, gutsy young women who wanted to rewrite the rules of work but weren't Cosmo-swilling *Sex and the City* wannabes or briefcase-toting empty-nesters with enough money to finance both a career change and a time-share in Hawaii? Where were the books that took a realistic look at how the heck you could finagle the anti 9-to-5 life while broke, rather than feeding us woo-woo, chakra-spinning visualization techniques and daily affirmations? After all, if you can't afford a box of crackers, you probably aren't going to love what you do for long.

I'm not an MBA or CPA or lawyer or financial planner. Nor am I a career coach. (Though I do seem to be the go-to gal in my circle of friends for advice on how to negotiate a project contract or how to tell their boss they'd like to slap him or her upside the head.) What I am is a gal who has been there and faxed that and can tell you what I've learned the hard way about how to work outside the 9-to-5 realm without winding up on food stamps. The way I see it, you might as well learn from my mistakes and save yourself some time, migraines, and credit card debt. If you want accredited legal and financial advice, though, you'd best consult a professional or hit up your lawyer cousin for a freebie.

That said, when I was asked to do this book, I realized I didn't want to just rely on my own experiences as a freelancer, freeloader, telecommuter, temp, and fan of all things flex. So I hit the books, scoured the web, and picked the brains of multiple career coaches, business experts, and trendwatchers. And I talked to dozens of twenty- and thirtysomething women across the country with self-styled careers or ambitions. I also squeezed in a couple chats with midlifers who have careers too fascinating not to savor. Many of these women are single, some are shacked up, and some have kids to boot. You'll find lots of their stories and suggestions woven into these pages.

No matter what their stage of life, these artists, activists, moonlighters, globetrotters, adrenaline junkies, burned-out execs, small-business owners, and aspiring superstars share the same sentiment: Quality of life trumps all else. Or as Molly Kenny, who founded a nonprofit yoga studio that serves the physically and emotionally challenged, puts it, "As far as we know, you only go around once, and I am hell-bent on not having a mediocre life." If you, too, are looking for a less cringe-inducing way to make a buck, balance a side gig or family with your day job, or crash though the glass ceiling, you've come to the right place.

You don't need me to tell you this isn't your mother's career—the days of segregated want ads, job titles like "Gal Friday," and high school guidance counselors pushing applications for colleges that attract "marriageable" men in premed are light-years behind us. Now that everyone's wired to the hilt and company loyalty, pension plans, social security, and the eight-hour workday are pretty much a historical footnote, we're far more enterprising than our parents ever were. Multiple career changes, extended travel, and entrepreneurship are de rigueur. "It's not like you get out of school and say, 'Okay, what's my forty-year game plan?'" says Kirsten Johnson, a career counselor to other twentysomethings and author of the blog Dream Big.

Still, parents, guidance counselors, and friends who've drunk the 9-to-5 Kool-Aid and are notoriously slow on the uptake can be prone to dispensing horrifically irrelevant advice. Even if they can get past pushing the MD-ESQ-MBA troika on you, they may advise you to do something as hapless as wearing a suit to a job interview on a construction site.

That's where this book comes in. I'll tell you how to research your dream job, find like-minded women to conspire with, and scrimp and save so you don't have to wait till you're sixty-five (or, worse, seventy-five) to do what you really want to do with your life. This is not an exhaustive guide, but a primer you can use as a jumping-off point—whether you want to pursue a career in carpentry, start your own dog-walking business, or finally make some headway on that novel you've been pretending to write for the past five years.

There's a lot here, so you may want to roll up your sleeves and get out your pen and notepad, or at least a pile of stickies. In fact, you may want to throw this book in your tote or backpack and take it with you on library or café research jaunts. (Hell, take it to your informational interviews, in case you need to revisit the rules on the care and feeding of your mentors.)

Know that unless you were born into royalty, you may have to make a long-range plan, even if it means crawling back into the cube for a couple years before you can escape from it. Believe me, you're not the only one who's ever had a savings account or resume deficit—I've been there, too, and lived to tell. And now I'm here to tell you that ditching the dream because you want immediate gratification is what's known as wimping out. Yes, it will take some hustling, chutzpah, and hard work to make a career change, but it can be done. Lest you feel unmotivated or overwhelmed, I've provided a handy-dandy "Show Me the Money" section and an "Anti 9-to-5 Action Plan" at the end of each chapter to give you a nudge in the right direction.

None of this is to say you shouldn't work a traditional 9-to-5 office job if you want to. After all, if it ain't broke, why fix it? But since you picked up this book, I'm going to assume you're at least a little bit anti-curious. The following pages will tell you what your work life could be like in the DIY-career trenches—the good, the bad, and the ugly. So take a peek outside your cube and see what you think. Because, when all is said and done, life's too short to stress about work when you're sleeping.

Part I

MAKE your MOVE

chapter 1

→ I WANT
to find a
CAREER
I'm really
* Passionate
about

"Human beings were not meant to sit in little cubicles staring at

computer screens all day, filling out useless forms and listening

to eight different bosses drone on about mission statements."

—Ron Livingston as Peter Gibbons in *Office Space,* 1999

When I decided to flee the cube in my mid-twenties, I knew I wanted to do something related to writing, but I had no idea what. How I would get from point A (gainfully employed by someone else) to point B (gainfully self-employed) was a mystery. But instead of giving any of this an ounce of forethought, I blindly leapt into the anti 9-to-5 chasm. You might say I was all madness and no method.

The year was 1992. Back then, if you wanted online advice, you had to post a question to Usenet (an ancient computer network that predates the web). Since I didn't know what Usenet was (and still can't really tell you what it is), many of my questions about self-employment went unanswered. Occasionally I'd go to chamber of commerce mixers in an attempt to glean advice or maybe even a client, but I was shy as hell, I didn't know what I was doing, and I stuck out like a sore thumb among all those well-groomed *adults.* Once in a while a friend who felt sorry for me would give me the name of a family member's cousin twice removed who worked as a newspaper reporter or obscure book author, someone three decades older who said I could pick their brain. I'd call, and they'd gripe about what a rotten career writing was and encourage me to run for the hills at top speed.

So I fumbled and bumbled through the first few years of my so-called freelance career the best I could, bouncing from freelance jobs to temp jobs to part-time jobs and back again. Sometimes I'd say the wrong thing in meetings, or choke on my hamburger right as a potential client asked about my qualifications. Often I undercharged for my work, lived beyond my (already meager) means, and bounced my rent checks.

Once I'd mercifully put this groping-in-the-dark phase behind me, I realized I had learned a heck of a lot about carving out a self-styled solo career—and that I had made it so very hard on myself by not investigating and preparing for what I was getting into first.

That's where this book comes in. My rocky transition from employee to my own employer is not one I would recommend to my worst enemy. But I've since amassed a load of know-how about making people want to hire me—at a living wage, no less—and swapped war stories with dozens of other women who have successfully left behind the 9-to-5 grind. And I'd love to be the one who prevents you from making the same dumb mistakes I made.

If you know you want out of the cube but have no idea what your next move is, this chapter is for you. Even if you do have a career path in mind, this chapter will steer you toward some invaluable resources for scouting it out.

DO YOU HAVE TO LOVE YOUR JOB?

Of course not. In the course of writing this book, I talked to plenty of women who are happy to just collect a paycheck at some bland mercenary gig and pursue the projects they can really sink their teeth into after hours. But for every one of those women, I talked to a dozen cube-dwellers who said they'd prefer to earn their keep some way other than by wading through an inbox, snoring through staff meetings, and covering their boss's derriere.

5

Some, like Andrea Beyer of Seattle, crave a less stodgy, more stimulating work environment—one less inclined to cause narcolepsy. "I was tired of emailing people who sat next to me, tired of meetings that accomplished nothing," says the thirty-year-old, who left a high-profile corporate gig after three years to temp by day and learn to cut and color hair by night. "I just wanted to be more active, not so sedentary in front of the computer." She also wanted a job with more flexible hours, one that involved helping people feel good about themselves, rather than helping a department head meet some arbitrary "bottom line."

Others, like Gwynn Cassidy of Manhattan, hanker for more meaningful work. After running a beauty and lifestyle channel for a well-known website—complete with cushy office, free makeup, and A-list parties—the thirty-five-year-old came to the conclusion that "there's only so much writing you can do about mascara and lip gloss before you lose it." After giving five years of her life to "interviews about Botox and teenage acne," Gwynn began immersing herself in her local feminist community. Today she juggles a part-time telecommuting gig for the National Organization for Women with running the nonprofit she cofounded, Girls in Government, which encourages young women to accept leadership roles.

Still others, like Kate Greenen of Detroit, who's twenty-five and has worked in what she calls "the lucrative world of financial planning" since age twenty-one, find themselves asking with alarming frequency, *Is this all there is?* "I've been offered training, stability, and fantastic benefits," says Kate, who plans to sell everything she owns and get a marriage and family counseling graduate degree. "But I started *really* hating getting up. Life lost color—I was always searching for something fun to do or I was out shopping. Earn, consume, die. It was a soul-sucking circle. After years of bitching about paperwork in an industry that held absolutely no interest for me, I'd rather be broke than on the earning-spending-consuming hamster wheel."

Andrea, Gwynn, and Kate are hardly anomalies. Countless women log hour after hour in their cubes while dreaming of the day they can escape to a more fulfilling gig. In fact, a 2005 study by a leading business research group found that only half of all working Americans are happy with their jobs. And a 2006 CareerBuilder.com poll found that 53 percent of America's gainfully employed consider their coworkers, well, "a bunch of monkeys." The big question is why, in a society where most of us spend roughly 1,800 hours a year at work, do we stick it out at tedious day jobs that make our palms itch and our eyes bleed?

For one thing, most of us are hip to the fact that eating out of Dumpsters is overrated. Not getting paid is simply not an option, no matter how tempting it is to pull a Peter Gibbons (of *Office Space* fame) and stop showing up to work. What's more, many of us are methodically chipping away at student loans, saving our beans for that Eurailpass we've been fantasizing about, or stockpiling our savings till the day we can afford to hang our own shingle. Others are learning the ropes in an industry they hope to one day take by storm. Or actively interviewing for brighter, shinier jobs—ones that might even give us our own offices. With a window. And a door that locks.

Yet some of us are biding our time in our current dead-end gigs till that six-figure book deal or winning Lotto ticket falls out of the sky. And some of us aren't sure how we wound up in our cubicles or server aprons in the first place, much less where we should go next. If the latter scenarios ring a bell, take heart. Life in the cube doesn't have to last forever. This book will tell you how to make your way to the nearest exit.

WHAT'S YOUR COSMETOLOGY SCHOOL?

At a recent mind-numbing temp gig, my fellow short-timers and I gathered 'round the color copier to swap ghost stories of day gigs past. Trying to top each other's terrifying tales of subordination, termination, and humiliation soon gave way to true confessions of What We Really Want to Do with Our Lives. My friend Andrea was putting herself through cosmetology school during nights and weekends. Another officemate (let's call her Roz) worked four "tens" and used her Fridays off to get her home-based retail business off the ground. I, too, fessed up about my alter ego, who wrote essays and articles on the bus, during lunch, and in the wee morning hours.

The only one who remained silent was a guy I'll call George, a gung-ho, flat-topped ex-marine whose thirty-five-hour-a-week temp gig consisted of compiling some stats for a couple hours each morning, and, well, that was pretty much it. His boss hadn't given him enough to do, despite George's repeated requests for a heavier workload. Bored silly, ol' Geo would spend the rest of each day drumming his fingers on his desk, periodically reading aloud the headlines from CNN.com until 5 PM rolled around. Suffice it to say, we were all itching for him to land a more stimulating gig.

"See, I need to do what all of you are doing," George finally chimed in. "I need to come up with a career I can actually get behind. But what's *my* cosmetology school? I need to figure that out."

While I had a hard time envisioning even the figurative George pursuing a career in hair and makeup, I appreciated the sentiment. His question—"What's *my* cosmetology school?"—pretty much said it all. He didn't want to just collect a paycheck; he wanted a job that would make him feel useful, energized, like he was more than an organ-grinding monkey. If, like George, you have no idea what your beauty school is, don't despair. Though hardly an overnight process, identifying it is something anyone with the ability to daydream and write lists can do.

Of course, lists are only the beginning. From there, you'll need to investigate what landing your dream gig entails. But let's take this one step at a time. The first order of business is figuring out exactly what the heck it is you'd like to do with your life. If the only thing that comes to mind is *Not this!* don't fret. In this section, you'll dig a little deeper until you unearth some concrete answers.

Step 1: Go to your happy place.

Is there somewhere you do your best brainstorming (preferably away from your place of employment)? It doesn't matter if it's the can, the bus, the gym, the mall, or Costa Rica. The idea is to retreat from your cubicle to a place where you can think uninterrupted for an hour or more. Make sure you bring a pen and paper, or a laptop, with you. Whether it takes a lunch hour or a couple Saturday mornings, you're going to keep brainstorming until the blank page you started with is crammed with ideas.

Step 2: Thumb through your mental scrapbook.

You've probably heard it said that you should take inventory of every work-related and recreational activity you've done since you were the ripe old age of, say, six—from classes, hobbies, and clubs to jobs, internships, and volunteer gigs. The idea, say "those self-helpy parachute books," as a few women I talked to called them, is to note the activities you've enjoyed, no matter how small or fleeting.

For example, I used to love to draw when I was a kid, and I took all kinds of art classes at the Y. I must have subjected my poor parents to about 200 variations of the same sunset/mountainscape scene (drawn in those messy pastels that get all over your hands and clothes), which they dutifully oohed and ahhed over. The bad art continued all through high school, and by the time I reached college, there was no doubt in my mind I wanted to pursue a career in "uh, something arty." And now here I am, making stuff for a living, though I'm happy to report you won't find any badly drawn sunsets in my portfolio (maybe just some horrible poetry).

What did I love to do as a kid? Your first stop on this trip down Memory Lane should be your own childhood, from those endless Saturday afternoons spent inventing stuff to playing Wonder Woman and otherwise saving the world in your basement or back yard. Maybe you ran the lemonade-and-cookie empire on the corner. Or outfitted the family dog, cat, and gerbil in gold lamé. Or directed all the neighborhood kids in elaborate productions of *Hairspray*.

When you stumble on your own "Oh, yeah—I really liked doing that," write it down, even if it's some obscure task you only did once for half an hour, like fixing your Luddite father's computer when it crashed. Then ask yourself *why* this satisfied you so much. Was it the saving-another-person's-ass thing that made you feel good? Did you revel in the problem-solving? Or are you just one of those gadget whizzes who salivates over all things digital?

Or, if revisiting every nook and cranny of the first two or three decades of your life is too overwhelming, the remaining questions in this section can help you cut to the chase.

What do I want to learn next? Many entrepreneurs I talked to said they considered their past 9-to-5 jobs "school," only without the zits and homework. Taking gigs that teach you new skills or introduce you to people you want to meet is like "getting paid to get an education," says Michelle Madhok of Manhattan, the thirty-four-year-old founder of the shopping website SheFinds.com. For example, Michelle wanted to improve her public-speaking skills, so at her previous job she volunteered to give a lot of presentations.

But maybe, like most people, you fear giving PowerPoint presentations more than death. Maybe instead, like Maggie Kleinpeter of Baton Rouge, you have an art degree, are crafty as hell, and aspire to work for yourself one day. Unfortunately, you have the business sense of a cocker spaniel. So, like Maggie did before starting Supermaggie, her online mecca of silkscreened tees and other girlie goodies, you spend several years working for a tiny greeting-card company (or your industry of choice), where you can learn the ropes of running your own show. "That job was probably the best possible job to have because the owners pretty much showed me how to run a business," the thirty-year-old says. By the time Maggie walked away from this paid education, she knew how to talk to customers, market a product, contact wholesalers and retailers, work a trade show, and then some.

But what if you're not sure what you want to learn next? With so much virgin territory before you, the real question is, How *could* you be sure? When trying to figure out your next career move, dabbling is the name of the game. You can work in a dive shop and learn to scuba, like my friend Danielle did for a year. (Her consensus: Diving rocks; retail, not so much.) You can volunteer for a crisis hotline to see what you think of counseling domestic-violence victims, like I did in my twenties. (Intense, but rewarding; still, not the ultimate career path for me.) You can intern on an organic farm to see if country living agrees with you, get your EMT license and try your hand at rescue work, and on and on and on. Think of this period as an opportunity, like those electives you took in high school or college (wood shop, anyone?), but with performance reviews instead of report cards.

When was I at the top of my game? Take a second look at those projects, jobs, travels, and other peak experiences that made you feel like you could do no wrong, suggests career coach Kirsten Johnson. Coproducing *The Vagina Monologues* in college to raise money for local women's shelters gave her a sense of accomplishment unlike anything she did before or since.

Even if you don't have some short-lived apprenticeship with a Jedi master, far-flung Peace Corps adventure, or near brush with fortune and fame in your closet, surely there must be some past event that you occasionally replay in your mind when life at the computer monitor or espresso machine is about as exciting as watching golf on TV. (Of course, if you peaked drinking Coronas in Mexico on spring break, you may be hard pressed to find anyone who will pay you to reprise that role.)

My dream job of yore was a volunteer gig walking dogs at my city's animal shelter—hardly glamorous, yet infinitely rewarding. The dogs were happy to get out of their cages, I was happy to get my mutt fix, and the city was happy to get some free labor. To me, that job was the Peace Corps of petcare.

What do I never want to do again as long as I live? This may seem obvious, but sometimes listing all the jobs and activities that you dread and detest—or have completely burned out on—can help solidify what your next move should be. Like many women I talked to, Molly Kenny, thirty-nine, a licensed speech therapist, had seen enough bureaucracy in her six years working at a hospital to last a lifetime. "Every thirty days you do progress reports and you have twenty-two cases, and you're spending all that time shuffling papers—even though there's not that much to say after a month," says Molly, who now runs the Samarya Center, a nonprofit yoga studio in Seattle that caters to seniors and people with special physical and emotional needs. Frustrated that she was spending far more time writing about people's health woes than helping to resolve them, Molly created her own gig in the health arena, one that's infinitely more hands on and less corporate.

Enough about me, what do you *think of me?* Sometimes brainstorming with a trusted pal or next of kin—that is, those who recognize that being a doctor or lawyer aren't your only viable career options—can be a big help. A pointed "When you envision me in my ideal job, what do you see?" can yield some unexpected yet helpful results, says Kirsten, the peer counselor. Since we women are so good at downplaying our strengths, sometimes it takes the peanut gallery to remind us we have said strengths in the first place. Sure, we all know what tasks we excel at on the job and what subjects we nailed in school, but maybe we don't *enjoy* those tasks or topics. Or maybe we fail to recognize that we also have a knack for (and a real love of) diplomacy or digital cameras or deciphering IKEA furniture instructions.

My friend Maria, who's utterly fried after a decade of social work, is trying this "What do you think I should do with my life?" tactic now. She's open to any and all suggestions for new career paths to explore on the side and hopefully transition into. Since she's the biggest Martha Stewart I know (she has runners and a candelabra on her dining room table; need I say more?), she's been hearing a lot of suggestions revolving around interior design, event planning, and horticulture.

A hardcore gardener, Maria's really taken to this last suggestion. Last I checked with her, she was acing her exams in a botany class at the local university and had already lined up three friends with back yards she could practice her budding landscape-design talents on.

Step 3: Play location scout.

Exploring what you want to do for a living is only half the equation. There are also such variables as when, where, and how you want to do it, and with whom. Working in a physical setting and culture that won't make you gnash your teeth or twitch uncontrollably is equally important as doing a job you can stomach fifteen, twenty-five, or forty hours a week. For example, if you're an outdoor fanatic who hyperventilates at the mere thought of recycled air, why on earth would you interview at a labyrinthine office complex devoid of opening windows?

"It's two issues," says Lisa Kivirist, author of *Kiss Off Corporate America: A Young Professional's Guide to Independence*. "What kind of job structure works for you, and what kind of work are you doing?" she asks. Kivirist, thirty-eight, who today runs an environmentally friendly bed-and-breakfast in Wisconsin and the Rural Renaissance Network, a group that educates people on sustainable country living, initially thought her beef with 9-to-5 life was just a dislike of the advertising industry she worked in. But trying to work for nonprofits proved it was going into an office eight hours a day that made her flesh crawl. In her new life as an innkeeper and back-to-the-land spokesperson, she enjoys doing many of the marketing-ish tasks she did at her traditional office jobs—she just does them from home now.

Determining whether you're most comfortable working in your latest Salvation Army find at a funky boutique, in workboots as part of a roadwork crew, or in bed in your skivvies, perched over your laptop, is only part of it. Do you see yourself at a desk, becoming at one with the headset and computer screen, or on your feet, perhaps teaching, healing, selling, serving, making stuff, studying a petri dish, or operating heavy machinery? Do you want to work with kids,

13

Career quiz for women who can't stand career quizzes

If you've got half a brain, you'll find those "What Type of Job Is Right for Me?" quizzes on the web about as useful as your weekly horoscope. How you really feel about sharing a four-by-six-foot space with a hygienically challenged, socially stunted coworker usually has zilch to do with the meager multiple-choice options these tests offer. Yes, you may get affirmation that you like to help people, work with power tools, or swing from a trapeze, but you'll still need to research and test-drive any new career you're thinking of pursuing.

"'What are your values?' seems to me a much more important question," says peer counselor Kirsten Johnson. If your interests or values are still a little hazy after working through this chapter, chew on these questions awhile, and I suspect those values will start to crystallize in no time. To illustrate, I've offered up my own (wildly embarrassing) answers.

1. What's on your nightstand? What books and magazines you're reading can be pretty telling about what turns your crank. (As an example, my nightstand's brimming with issues of *The Bark,* my favorite dog magazine; *Swivel,* a literary journal of women's humor writing; and whatever book about tortured adolescence I'm currently reading— at the moment, *The Liars' Club*—all of which could lead one to speculate that I'm a witty dog owner with a fair amount of baggage. Perhaps, though, your nightstand runneth over with a couple dozen issues of *National Geographic* and *Shutterbug,* in which case I'd wager that you're a travel-photography buff.)

2. Out of all your friends' jobs, which one are you most jealous of? Why? (I'm most jealous of the dog-walkers I know. They spend their days getting the blood pumping, getting muddy, and interacting with colleagues who are always happy to see them. What's not to love?)

3. What's the one thing you've been talking about doing forever that your friends are sick of hearing about? (Guess. If stumped, see above.)

4. What's the one off-the-wall, pie-in-the-sky job you've always wanted to try that no one knows about? (I have this fantasy where I get hired to work as a personal assistant to a lavishly wealthy person. I swear. Maybe some Hollywood debutante with a $13 million estate overlooking the Pacific who just keeps me around so I can run her errands, schedule her spa appointments, and weigh in on how great her emaciated butt looks in her new $350 jeans.)

5. If you could start any business or organization, or sell any service or ware, what would it be? (Um, books?)

6. If you could work anywhere in the world, in any country or organization, where would it be? Doing what? (Writing, in some ancient European farmhouse. With a personal chef on hand. And a hot tub out back.)

7. If "debt," "years," and "practical" weren't words in your vocabulary, what would you be doing now—besides sipping margaritas on your own tropical island? (This.)

Obviously, some of my "values" (personal chef? hot tub? hello?) won't point me toward any moneymaking ventures anytime soon, but there's some useful information in here: For starters, if this writing thing doesn't pan out, I may want to look into working with dogs, since apparently I think about them morning, noon, and night. What's more, I may want to explore what being a personal assistant actually entails, since I have evidently romanticized that career choice to the hilt. And finally—thank god for small miracles—I'm happy in my current incarnation as a writer.

You get the idea. Now see where this little daydreaming exercise takes you.

animals, the general public, the underprivileged, or businesspeople? Do you want nights or days off? A full-time job or a couple part-time ones? A commute to the next room or the next city? And so on.

If you're not sure yet, don't worry. The rest of this book—and the research you're about to embark on—will help you answer all these questions and then some.

START SUSSING OUT THE GIGS

When you can rattle off at least five tasks you'd like to do in exchange for cold, hard cash, and some characteristics of the work environment you see yourself in, it's time to start figuring out how you can parlay the ideas you've written down into actual jobs that people get paid to do. Don't be afraid to get outlandish. At this stage, no idea is too nuts.

Even if you've already started researching the jobs that are out there for, say, iguana-lovers, and how much money a vet assistant, zoologist, or pet-sitter can make, let me suggest a few resources— online and off—you won't want to skip. While scouting out the gigs, pay attention to everything from work environment, industry culture, and office hours to salary, education and skills required, and job-market outlook. Also note the names and contact info of any up-and-coming hotshots in the field whose footsteps you'd love to follow in (and brains you'd love to pick). You're going to need them when you get to the next chapter.

Know that when I say "research," I'm not just talking about reading one article or emailing one person in the field and calling it a day. If you don't do the necessary detective work, you may wind up just as miserable in a new vocation as you are in your current one. Having profiled a number of women in careers I previously knew nothing about, I can tell you it's not too hard to get your arms around the nuts and bolts of a new vocation in a short period of time. One day of scouring the web or camping out at the library can make the difference between having no idea about what you're getting yourself into and being reasonably well informed.

Note to naysayers: Before you write off being a pilot, politician, or pastry chef as impractical, pretend for a moment that you don't have student loans, rent, dependents, or anything else tying you down. Also, never mind your as-yet-unproven ideas about how much things cost or how long they take, like getting another degree, government aid, paying customers, or a promotion. We'll get to all these later in the book. And by all means, forget about what your mother would say. You're the one who will be punching the clock in your illustrious new profession, not her.

Okay, so, got your pen and notebook handy? Let's get this recon mission started.

Yellow Pages. Suppose, like every other person in the country, you want to work with animals. (It's not just me, is it?) Under "Pets" in the Yellow Pages, you'll likely find pet-sitters, -walkers, trainers, photographers, groomers, taxi services, supply shops, shelters, therapists, psychics, and poop-scoopers—and we haven't even gotten to the vet, zoo, and wildlife sanctuary listings yet. You can use all these businesses to learn more about what kind of work is out there for, say, an iguana-lover like you. How? By visiting their websites, signing up for their newsletters, checking out their offices, and talking to their employees.

Occupational reference guides. Though somewhat staid, the free, online *Dictionary of Occupational Titles* (www.occupationalinfo.org) is always good for job ideas, not to mention glossary definitions of everything from a French binding to a frothing machine (yeah, I had no idea what these were either). The U.S. Department of Labor's Occupational Outlook Handbook (www.bls.gov/oco), with its invaluable details on necessary training, possible salary, and job-market outlook for hundreds of careers, may also help. And if you've got $25 to spare, the *Career Pathways Handbook* and *Career Pathways: Your Guide to the Top 100 Careers* (www.cassio.com) add to the mix profiles of people doing the actual jobs.

Websites for job-seekers. Happily, sites like CareerBuilder.com, Monster.com, and Vault.com do more than just warehouse reams of resumes and job listings. They also feature profiles on what it's like to be everything from a food scientist to a smoke jumper to a tattoo artist, as well as a bevy of advice on how to become one.

Professional organizations. A Google search on "women firefighters" turns up Women in the Fire Service, Inc., an organization that, as you might guess, helps women curious about or currently working in firefighting. The group's website features pages galore about the history of women firefighters, the difference between structural (city) and wildland (forest) firefighting, training and testing requirements for firefighters, details on how to apply to a fire station, recommended books and articles, job openings, event listings, industry news, a message board for advice-seekers, and links to a jillion other relevant sites—priceless information for any gal thinking of donning a helmet and turnouts.

Many professional organizations also offer free e-newsletters and hold regional meetings, both of which you should absolutely take advantage of. Not only will these groups clue you in to the latest advancements, laws, and political campaigns affecting the field, but many—like WashTech and the National Writers Union—advocate for their members.

Online communities. Countless web communities, from the Seattle Writergrrls to DigitalEve, have discussion lists and forums you can join for free and milk for information on industries and gigs you know zip about. Yahoo! Groups is another gold mine of information on careers ranging from bus drivers to flight attendants. And if you're looking for a more tried-and-true profession, check out the discussion boards on job-hunting sites like Monster.com, Vault.com, and SimplyHired.com.

The websites and blogs of people who share your interests. See someone on a discussion list or forum who seems to know something about your pet interest? If they have a website or blog, scour it for dirt on the job, industry culture, pay, highlights, and lowlights. In addition,

Google your pet topic plus "expert," and see who and what sites come up. Bonus points if you can get the person to give you some tips about breaking into their field. (More in the next chapter on scoring face time with those in the know.)

Books, newspapers, and magazines. Unplugging can be a beautiful thing (remember fresh air and interacting with real live *people?*). In bookstores, newsstands, and libraries, you're bound to find publications you didn't see or couldn't access online. You may even surprise yourself by gravitating to the plumbing or photography section first and wondering how you could someday make money at those vocations, instead of art history, which you thought was your interest du jour. Also keep an eye out for those "50 Best Jobs" cover stories in publications like *BusinessWeek, Entrepreneur,* and your local newspaper or metropolitan magazine.

ANTI 9 to 5 tip

This is probably a big fat "duh," but it bears mentioning. Salary ranges will vary with geographic location, employer, self-employment, and rung on the ladder. So if you don't see a salary breakdown for a particular career path you're investigating, don't assume that all computer programmers (or cabbies or clothing designers) will make that amount per year. Depending on the variables—which you'll suss out, of course—the pay may vary. For example, a carpenter in Trenton, New Jersey, with two years' experience makes an average salary of $41,000, while the same job in Tulsa, Oklahoma, earns an average salary of $35,000.

Salary sites. During the earlier brainstorming exercises, I told you not to worry about the money just yet. Well, here's your chance to play the realist: You officially have my permission to start thinking about salaries. After all, you need to know if your lifestyle and potential compensation in this new field will mesh (more on this at the end of the chapter). Sites like Salary.com, SalaryExpert.com, and the Department of Labor's National Compensation Survey (www.bls.gov/ncs) are good places to start.

SHOULD I GO BACK TO SCHOOL?

That depends. Signing up for tens of thousands of dollars in grad-school debt because you're sick of asking, "Paper or plastic?" eight hours a day is a pretty pricey stopgap. "It's not like once you get the degree, you get the job," says Beena Ahmad, a twenty-seven-year-old Brooklyn resident who's wrestled with whether to attend law school.

So before you take the GRE, pack all your worldly possessions into a VW bus, and head off to Los Angeles, make sure you can see yourself eating, living, and breathing the topic in question for the next several years. Take a page from Kate, the financial planning administrator turned would-be family counselor: Volunteer in the industry first to see if the pros outweigh the cons. Peruse the syllabi and textbooks you'll be spending untold thousands to become intimately acquainted with. Audit a couple classes to see if the field holds your interest once there's bona fide homework involved.

If the industry you're considering doesn't require that you memorize thirty-seven technical tomes and ace a stack of grueling certification exams, you'd still be wise to test-drive the topic with a couple of classes. Besides giving you a taste, enrolling in a course or two can help you beef up your resume and meet others already working in the field—good comrades to have on your side. You don't have to blow a wad at a university, either; community colleges and other continuing-education centers will do just fine.

SHOULD I HIRE A CAREER COACH?

Hiring a coach to usher you through a career change is like hiring a personal trainer to help you get buff. You're forking over the cash for a cheerleader who knows more than you about the wonderful work of work and threatens to check up on your progress, so of course you're going to follow through.

Thing is, career coaches (a.k.a. career counselors, life coaches, or life architects) cost money, and unless you're one of the lucky few with a savings account burning a hole in her bra, it may seem as ludicrous as renting a limo to drive you to work—especially when, with a little research, schmoozing, and discipline, you can accomplish the same goals yourself. (If you're rusty on any of these fronts, not to worry. We'll talk about them all in the next two chapters.)

I say unless you're loaded, at the top of the workplace food chain, or plagued with some particularly sticky issues—like butting heads with a hellish boss who makes Miranda Priestly from *The Devil Wears Prada* look like a blind, three-legged kitten, or failing to get a nibble on your resume for eighteen straight months—just tap your friend who works in human resources, your neighbor the traveling sales guy, or your aunt who runs her own twenty-five-employee business. These people usually have a better handle on workplace dynamics than the rest of us.

If you do decide to go the coach route, know this: Since there's no governing board, anyone can call herself a career coach. And while there are many seasoned, talented coaches out there with all sorts of HR and management experience, psychology degrees, and books bearing their name, there are just as many quacks whose idea of a proactive career move is visualizing themselves into a promotion. In other words, get references, and don't hire anyone who requires you to prepay for umpteen sessions.

THE BEAUTY OF TRANSITIONING

Making photocopies for peanuts might be easier to swallow when you're fresh out of school and have nowhere to go but up. But what if, like the majority of twentysomethings, you can't afford a peanut butter sandwich, much less a pay cut or a third job? Or what if you're thirty or thirty-five, saddled with a mortgage and mouths to feed, and have a tough time wrapping your head (and wallet) around the idea of starting over again?

That's when long-range goals come in handy. As Anya Kamenetz writes in *Generation Debt: Why Now Is a Terrible Time to Be Young*, when it comes to career dreams and financial realities, sometimes you have to "adjust to your reality." The beauty of a transition plan is that you get to keep your current gig and paycheck while doing the research, sampling new industries, even testing the market for your kitchen-table-business idea. If you realize the life of a tattoo artist or paramedic isn't your bag, you can bail without horrific financial repercussions.

Even if it takes you three to five years to transition from crappy career A to shiny career B, you'll be happier devoting two, five, or twenty hours a week to a long-range plan than moping month after month about how you hate your cube-monkey existence. (Your friends, who are no doubt sick of hearing you whine, will be too.) Yes, life will be more hectic, and you may have to sacrifice your beloved TV time and vintage-handbag addiction, but getting off your duff can be energizing and empowering. Besides, it gives you something to look forward to during those agonizing 3 PM staff meetings.

Once you've identified how much training and volunteer experience the career you covet will require, you can make a realistic timetable of how long the transition will take. Your next step is to create a weekly to-do list of small, tangible tasks—for example, "Call three forensic scientists I worship to pick their brains"—so you feel like you're moving forward. Chapter 3 gets into more detail about how you can beat your inner slacker into submission, squeeze additional time from a cramped schedule, and stay motivated.

SHOW ME THE MONEY

How much money you need to live, and what lifestyle changes you're willing to make to meet your career goals, should factor into your transition plan too, especially if a starting salary in your new career isn't going to be as lucrative as your current day job.

Your first step is to create a realistic monthly budget. If you don't know how much you spend, start with all the usual monthly expenses—rent, cell phone bill, coffee habit—and then carry a notebook around with you for a week or two and write down where all your cash goes. Resist the temptation to cheat, including any and all vices, from shoes to cigarettes. If you're planning a vacation six months down the line that will cost $750 or are pretty sure you're going to splurge on that $150 dress you tried on over the weekend, divide that by twelve and tack it on to your monthly expenses.

If you have a problem with bounced checks (and all the pricey bank charges that come with them), it's time to start troubleshooting. Sign up for overdraft protection on your checking account. Scrap your commercial bank account for a credit union one—they're often cheaper and have better interest rates. And if you don't know how to balance your checkbook, learn. If a former financial moron like me can do it, so can you.

Late bill payments have got to go, too. You're risking pricey interest rate increases on your credit cards and reinstatement fees from your utility companies, not to mention jeopardizing your credit rating. If you're in big debt, now might be a good time to cut up your credit cards and consult a nonprofit credit consolidation service like Consumer Credit Counseling Service (CCCS) or Money Management International (MMI), both available at MoneyManagement.org.

And if you're living beyond your means, it's last call, my friend, and high time you took a long, hard look at your lifestyle. If changing careers is enough of a priority for you, you'll start downsizing ASAP. Consider it your personal fuck you to big business and all the cookie-cutter merchandise they're trying to shove down the throat of every freethinking twentysomething female in the country. "Buying stuff and getting into debt is never going to be rebellious," *Generation Debt* author Anya Kamenetz assures me. "*Not* buying is rebellious."

Making your own lunch and lattes and scaling back on your text-messaging habit is only the beginning. I'm not suggesting you live like a monk or sleep on a subway grate to finance a career change, but any big-ticket items you can jettison from your monthly expenses can help. For starters, try bartering with your landlord or roommates: Can you mow the lawn or take on some additional household chores for a reduction in rent? Can you lower your car insurance, get a smaller apartment, or take in more roommates? How about trading in your car for a bike and bus pass, or moving to a city where one month's rent isn't the equivalent of the gross national product of a Third World nation? If you're willing to scrimp and save now, you can shave months, even years, off your long-range transition plan. And you can enjoy the luxury of not worrying so much about how you're going to make rent.

ANTI 9-TO-5 ACTION PLAN

We've covered a lot of ground in this first chapter. To make your transition plan less daunting, let's break it down into stages. Depending on how much free time you have, each stage might last a week, a month, or maybe more. The stages may overlap, too. Give yourself a realistic date when you'll begin each stage. I recommend starting Stage 1 today, Stage 2 two weeks from now, and so on, to keep the momentum. If this is far too ambitious for your schedule, spread each stage out by a month or two. Do your best to take at least three steps a week, even if you only spend fifteen minutes on all three.

STAGE 1: TAKE THE COSMETOLOGY SCHOOL TEST	
Start date	**Checklist**
	Brainstorm time! Jot down any activities, jobs, classes, or volunteer stints you've enjoyed to date, even if you were seven at the time.
	Also write down those skills you're itching to learn, tasks you want to avoid like the plague, and suggestions from like-minded friends or family.
	Think long and hard about—and then note in your trusty notepad—the type of setting and culture you want to work in.

STAGE 2: DO THE RECON	
Start date	**Checklist**
	Start scouring the web and library for actual jobs that match up with the interests you identified in Stage 1.
	Suss out the salaries of the jobs and fields you're most excited about.
	As you play detective, keep your eyes out for up-and-comers in your dream gig. Save their names and contact info.
	Take a class on the field or topic you're most jazzed about. If you're considering grad school, take one or two more classes and peruse relevant syllabi and reference books.

STAGE 3: GET YOUR MONEY STRAIGHT	
Start date	Checklist
	Figure out—honestly—how much you spend each month on living expenses, debt, and fun.
	Scrutinize your lifestyle. What expenses and vices can you jettison? Vow to ditch at least one today.
	If you're prone to bouncing checks and racking up late-payment fees, get a grip. See "Show Me the Money" on page 23 for ideas.
	If your credit card debt is out of control, consider consolidating through an organization like Consumer Credit Counseling Service (CCCS).

STAGE 4: START PLOTTING YOUR TRANSITION	
Start date	Checklist
	Think about whether you'll need to move to another city or state to pursue your dream gig (or to cut down on living expenses).
	Once you have a firmer grasp on your cash and the training your dream career requires, make a preliminary timeline of how long it will take you to get there.

chapter 2

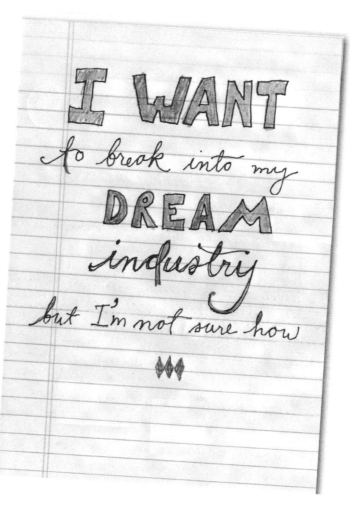

I WANT
to break into my
DREAM
industry
but I'm not sure how

"There is nothing more conducive to respect, trust, and honor in business

than quiet tastes—in clothes as in everything else. One instinctively respects

the young lady who is smartly attired in dark, simple clothes, ideally

adapted to the business environment. How much more sensible she looks,

how much more eager one is to trust her with confidential information,

with responsible duties, than the flippant person who wears gaudy clothes!"

—Book of Etiquette, Volume II, 1921

I met Betsy Anderson when she emailed me looking for advice on how to crack Seattle's freelance writing market. With a bachelor's degree in journalism from Western Washington University and a smidge of experience reporting for a suburban rag during college, she was itching to nab herself a magazine or newspaper starter job. When we first spoke on the phone, Betsy, who's twenty-five, was living with her parents in a Seattle suburb and working two part-time jobs to make ends meet: Starbucks barista and YMCA "member services rep." Because she's interested in criminal justice and investigative reporting, Betsy was also putting in twenty unpaid hours a week as an investigative intern at the Seattle Public Defender's Office, where she helped lawyers interview witnesses, perform criminal background checks, and crank out legal briefs.

I soon learned I was one of a dozen or so working writers Betsy had pinged for career tips. Not only that, she was systematically contacting every publication in town to get the scoop on job requirements—which, though far easier to do in Seattle than in, say, Manhattan, is still ambitious. In addition, this was her second three-month internship at a public defender's office, because, as she says, she's "the kind of person that is willing to go the extra mile, sacrifice money, et cetera, to get good foundational experience."

Sure, it's tough for Betsy to swallow her puny paychecks and the living-with- Mom-and-Dad thing, especially when many of her peers waltzed right into fast-cash career-track gigs at neighboring tech empires like Microsoft and Nintendo. But Betsy wants a gig she can sink her teeth into, something that won't burn her out in two or three years. So she's boldly talking to everyone she can, getting the nitty-gritty experience to make her more attractive to publications like *Seattle* magazine, and making priceless contacts she can call on later for references or job leads.

This isn't to say all humble career beginnings require a sob story of the "In my day, we mouse-clicked our fingers to the bone and worked nineteen-hour shifts in exchange for cases of Jolt cola and phantom stock options" variety. But if you want to escape the cube, you have to be willing to do the hard time—a process that can take anywhere from a few months to a few years, depending on how much moxie, savings, and room in your schedule you have. (Happily for Betsy, she nabbed a job as reporter at a weekly community newspaper a few months after we first talked. All that pavement-pounding paid off.)

The beauty of talking to people who've already climbed the ranks, and of sampling careers through starter gigs, is that you get to preview your fantasy career. It's like trying on a pair of jeans before pulling out your wallet, or checking that the toilet flushes before you sign the apartment lease. If you don't like what you see, you simply walk away. But if you do, you now have a road map for getting there, not to mention an armful of contacts and a tricked-out resume to make future employers (or clients) lick their lips.

So get out that research you did in Chapter 1 on those coveted companies, industry superstars, and professional associations. It's time to find some real-life answers to those burning questions about your new career, and to firmly wedge your foot in that ever-revolving door.

THE NEW GIRLS' CLUB

B ecause starting at the bottom can be so humbling (especially if it's your second time around), I highly recommend you *not* go it alone. Finding yourself some other women on the rise—in your chosen new vocation or otherwise—to share job-hunting tips and resources with can help ease the frustration and loneliness of attempting to make a career change.

Chances are, someone in your own social circle is helping perpetuate the new girls' club right now and empowering a bunch of women in the process. My friend Valerie, whom I can always count on to plan a monthly estrogen night on the town or an annual "no boys allowed" cabin retreat, is the perfect example. But her networking prowess doesn't stop with her social life. Before becoming a social studies teacher, Valerie worked at a high-profile arts foundation that was growing exponentially. When droves of new coworkers and consultants from a variety of industries and cities started showing up, many of them women of color, the females in Valerie's department instituted a monthly happy-hour club they called Diva Night. "It was like, 'It's a mean world—let's band together,'" Valerie says. The point was to share a few laughs outside the office and support each other as women and as minorities, personally and professionally.

Starting your own Diva Night, Estrogen Club, or whatever you want to call it is as simple as picking a quiet pub or café and inviting several female friends or colleagues you'd like to swap ideas and war stories with, no matter what field they work in. But don't stop there. To meet other enterprising divas in the professional world, you have to step beyond the sanctity of your inner circle.

Now, before you slam this book shut, hear me out: I know the idea of chatting up strangers at some industry schmoozefest may seem more horrific than being a *Fear Factor* contestant tasked with choking down a plate of sea cucumbers. I thought so too when I first struck out on my own as a freelancer. But it doesn't have to be that way.

When it comes to shooting the breeze with other working stiffs, there are no hazing rituals involved, no secret handshakes. Instead, networking is just like talking to the person next to you on a plane: *I heard that's a good book—are you liking it? Are you from San Francisco or just visiting? Wow, this six-hour delay blows.* Besides, you're going to start really small. Total baby steps. We're not talking about rubbing elbows with chamber of commerce members who wear pinstripes and pearls and are old enough to be your grandmother. We're talking low-stress schmoozing tactics, many of which double as investigations into new vocations.

Online profiles. It doesn't get much easier than using online social networks like LinkedIn, MySpace, and Facebook to flaunt your work experience and meet other professionals. Just make sure your Google trail is squeaky clean—in other words, no posting of photos from that go-go-dancing gig you had in college or your lost Vegas weekend. And resist the urge to use the name of someone you don't know (but whose profile you read in an online network) in an effort to nab an interview with his or her employer. A move like that will surely come back to haunt you.

Friends with benefits. If you have activist, artpreneur, or other enterprising friends, you probably get invited to at least a couple free art openings or low-cost fundraising benefits each year. Next time you do, grab a buddy and go. It's always easier to walk into the unknown with a sidekick. Take turns chatting up someone who's standing alone at the bar; they'll be grateful for the save. Have the friend who mailed you the invite in the first place introduce you to any hotshots you want to meet. Think of the experience as your networking training ground. And see additional schmoozing tips on page 34.

Charity case. Besides being one of the best ways to meet people whose work you admire, volunteering at a highly publicized event helps you gain experience in an industry where you have none. It's

When volunteering at an event, don't settle for behind-the-scenes grunt chores like folding programs or restocking the bathrooms with toilet paper. Ask to work on the front lines, greeting guests, assisting a hotshot event coordinator, or chaperoning featured speakers to and from the green room. If there aren't enough plum jobs to go around, trade with another volunteer partway through; most people aren't total job hogs.

also the stealth way to get into trade shows, conferences, fundraisers, business expos, and live performances you couldn't otherwise afford. And because you're working the event, you'll undoubtedly have about ninety-three conversation-starters at your disposal. If you're still interested in the field once the stardust settles, find yourself an ongoing volunteer gig to keep a finger in the pie.

The women's room. Okay, I snuck this one in here. But if you've already tried the previous suggestions, you're more than ready to mingle with the big girls. It's time you checked out, in the flesh, some of the professional associations you Googled in Chapter 1. Start with estrogen-specific groups—DigitalEve, Women in Real Estate, Wrench-Wielding Mamas, whatever. You might as well take advantage of the instant support system at your fingertips. Once you realize many of these groups hold free or nominally priced job fairs, lectures, and workshops, you'll race to their registration pages to sign up. Again, the built-in agenda of these events makes meeting people and asking questions infinitely easier than standing around for a couple hours at an unstructured happy hour while balancing a wine glass and a stack of business cards.

Like-minded schmooze groups. Whether you're into dalmatians or democrats, you're certainly not alone. Take advantage of the instant camaraderie social groups not necessarily related to earning one's keep have to offer, like the politically minded DrinkingLiberally.org and the crafty knitters of StitchNBitch.org. For one thing, it's good schmoozing practice. For another, it gives you a new venue for meeting women and men who might be able to help with your career quest.

"CAN I TAKE YOU TO COFFEE?"

In your real-world and online travels, you're bound to stumble upon complete strangers and friends of friends you suspect hold the keys to the kingdom of your new career. Add these to the list of "fascinating people whose brain I'd love to download" you started compiling back in Chapter I. Look for career superstars that are just a few years ahead of you in your dream field, or in an enviable position in a related field. People who haven't been in the workforce too, too long will be more approachable.

"You want someone who's familiar with the landscape for someone your age, and you want someone who's more likely to stick around for a little bit," says Alexandra Robbins, author of *Conquering Your Quarterlife Crisis: Advice from Twentysomethings Who Have Been There and Survived.* In other words, you want to talk to a peer who gets where you're coming from—professionally, socially, financially—not someone who was in school in the Nixon administration and already has one foot in the retirement pool.

As someone who gets a lot of "Can I ask you a few questions about freelance writing?" emails, I can tell you a short and sweet introductory note is least intrusive. If you can't find someone's email address on their company website, call their office (never their home, unless they gave you their blessing) and make your plea by phone, but make it quick. Tell your hero who you are and who you aspire to be, what kind of work you've done, and what you hope to learn from them.

Small talk for chronic introverts

For no-frills tips on surviving any schmoozing situation, from introductions to career idols to elevator run-ins with keynote speakers, Melissa Wadsworth, author of *Small Talk Savvy: Operator's Manual,* is full of useful tips. Aside from breathing into a paper bag if need be, here's what she recommends:

✎ *Prepare.* Craft a thirty-second elevator speech in advance so you're not caught off guard when someone asks what your story is. Behold: "Hi, I'm Michelle Goodman and I've been working in the scintillating world of computer software for the past decade, but I'm thinking of getting into magazine writing. Hence my presence tonight."

✎ *Ask questions.* People love to talk about themselves, so fire away. Some easy conversation-starters: *Are you friends with the artist? Do you work in* [fancy-pants industry that I covet] *too? How do you like it?* Next, talk about the space the event's being held in, the fact that you're wearing the same chartreuse sweater, and anything else you have in common. Don't worry about sounding like a Nobel Prize nominee; go for personable.

Many people will be more than happy to help out, provided they're not already working eighteen hours a day. Ask to set up a time for a short chat—and by short, I mean thirty minutes or so—at a time that works for them. Offer to buy them a quick lunch, or at least coffee (at a café that's around their corner, not yours). And do be flexible if all they can give you is an emailed response to a couple of questions or a fifteen-minute phone call.

Some people you contact might suggest you meet them at their office for a breezy deskside chat. Definitely take them up on this. You'll get a glimpse into their work world (and the chance to see whether everyone's pierced and tattooed, or a walking J.Crew ad).

Listen. Give your chatting companion a chance to respond; don't blitz her with questions John McLaughlin–style or jump in with your own assessment of the brilliant Roaring Twenties decor. Nor should you scan the room for someone more interesting to meet.

Connect. Before you stuff your business card into someone's hand, converse with her for a few minutes to see if there's a common interest, mutual friend, or way you can help each other professionally.

Mingle. There's no point in standing in the corner, talking to the same three or four people you came with (and talked to at the last event). The idea is to meet new people. Otherwise, you might as well be at some random bar.

Smile. Enthusiasm will get you far; acting like you need a higher dosage of Prozac won't. Be positive and upbeat, but not phony. Don't bitch, whine, moan, yawn, or viciously gossip.

Stay in touch. If you hit it off with someone, don't let her business card collect dust on your desk. Send her a nice note saying you enjoyed the chat and hope to see her at the next shindig. Or send her the hilarious article you mentioned about people who dance with their dogs, a job lead, or anything else that's polite, sane, and relevant. With any luck, she'll reciprocate.

Informational interviewing etiquette

To best endear yourself to your professional hero, show some respect. Under no circumstances should you be late or a no-show, which, believe it or not, people do all the time. And unless you're a neurosurgeon on call, turn off your cell phone. Always insist on paying for food and drinks. And keep an eye on the clock so you don't run over the allotted time (unless your subject green-lights this). Here are some more ways you can win over your hero and get the most from your meeting.

Dazzle, don't demand. Don't insist on a job, an introduction to your lunch date's boss, or a peek at her contact list. People like to help likable people, not ones they find brazenly rude. Only contact someone for an informational interview if you genuinely want to hear her pearls of wisdom. That said, I wholeheartedly encourage you to become chummy with your industry heroes should they hold the door open. If they tell you to keep in touch, keep in touch. If at the end of the meeting they tell you to shoot their manager an email, race to the nearest computer. Don't squander a break when it's handed to you on a silver platter.

Study up. Take the time to read about your industry insider and the organization she works for. "Basically, become their biggest fan. If you flatter them, they're going to be more likely to help," says quarterlife-crisis guru Alexandra Robbins. Start with your hero's company website and online bio. Do a web search for any recent press on her, her company, or the entire industry so you can compliment her on any recent successes. If you don't understand the industry lingo, sites like Wikipedia.org or AcronymFinder.com can help translate it into English. Learn enough so you can sound knowledgeable yet casual, as if you were telling your roommate what happened on the last episode of *Lost.*

Don't expect a brain dump. Arrive with four or five specific questions written down (in case your mind goes blank). Rather than asking sweeping questions like, "Tell me about being a web designer," probe for the fine-grained details you couldn't find with a Google search: What's a typical workday like for you? What are the drawbacks of your job? How long did it take to get where you are? Is a graduate degree necessary? With my background, would I have to start at the bottom again, or could I get in the door at a higher level?

Take copious notes. Jot down anything you don't want to forget. During her last job search, my sister Naomi, who has a degree in policy wonkism, went on more informational interviews than anyone I know. Because she's a wonk, she made a spreadsheet to track the dozens of conversations she was having, and another to track the umpteen job leads she collected along the way. Though the spreadsheet route may not be for you, do record whom you talked to when and what transpired. You'll thank yourself six weeks down the line when trying to remember whether the Pat emailing you about some hot new internship opening was a man or a woman.

Give thanks. I'm sure this sounds like a no-brainer, but I can't tell you how many strangers have emailed me their freelance writing questions, only to never send so much as a one-line note of gratitude after I've spent an hour typing out a reply. If someone gives you the time of day, email or snail-mail them a thank you note, just as you would for a "real" job interview. If you think this is a trivial matter, think again: A recent CareerBuilder.com survey found that 15 percent of hiring managers said they'd write off a job candidate who didn't send a post-interview thank you note.

ANTI 9-to-5 tip

We're all human, which means that we're all going to snort our coffee out our nose at some point or another. If this happens, don't panic. Mingling maven Melissa Wadsworth says it's best to just brush off the gaffe with some self-effacing humor, something like, "Whoa, I'm getting so excited hearing about your work that I momentarily lost all motor control." Let the person think that you're not easily rattled (even if you are), share a laugh, and then move on.

I like to watch

If you get the opportunity, spending a morning or day shadowing a pro on the job can give you an incredible window into a career you've had only fleeting glimpses of. Sarah Givner, a twenty-one-year-old Dartmouth grad who majored in history, aspires to become a doctor with her own practice (the self-employment aspect is as important to her as the profession). Before committing to the post-baccalaureate science program she's been dreading—"I haven't taken my sciences since high school!"—she shadowed a couple of doctors to see if she's up for the long haul, not to mention the student loans. Although watching a radiation oncologist work with cancer patients was emotionally grueling, given all the disease and despair she was suddenly privy to, she was not the least bit deterred. Instead, she says, "it was cool to be able to sit in and see how these machines work and see what port films [x-rays that verify a patient is correctly positioned during radiation treatment] are."

If you're a vocational or college student, or a recent grad, you're in a great position to shadow. Many professionals are happy to help career rookies because they remember how humbling it was to be faced with working in a fast-food chain if they didn't develop some viable skill. Your school's career center may already boast a shadowing or externship program to connect you with a willing professional. If not, or if those all-nighters during final exams are now a distant memory, ask friends, family, and contacts from your (now-burgeoning) Rolodex if they know someone with your dream career who might welcome an observer. Some workplaces or vocations have shadowing programs in place, no matter how informal. Fire stations, for example, often let would-be firefighters ride along on emergency calls.

If you do shadow a pro, dress the part; don't show up to your local firehouse clad in your best interview suit. And make sure the parameters are clear before the workday begins: how long you'll stay, whether you should play fly on the wall or help out, if there's anything special you should bring. As with informational interviews, don't overstay your welcome, do offer to buy lunch for the person who's so generously donating their time, and always send a thank you note, pronto.

A PEON'S SURVIVAL GUIDE:
FROM PHOTOCOPIES TO PLUM PROJECTS

Fast-forward twelve weeks, twelve months, however long you need to get yourself from your current frustrating work situation to the pearly gates of your new career. You've likely hit every industry event in town, amassed three trees' worth of business cards, and filled five notebooks with details about dream jobs. At some point during this spelunking expedition, you're going to land on a career path you want to give a shot.

If you've only been in the workforce a few years, you probably won't be landing a glamorous role as associate director of multimedia development at a mom-and-pop ad shop. Instead you'll be vying for that choice spot in the agency's reception area. It's at this point that you just have to "suck it up," as Sarah, the would-be med student, puts it, and sign on as intern, temp, or administrative assistant to get in the game. Yes, the initial pay and projects might leave something to be desired, but if you're savvy, you won't be answering phones for long.

"I hear people express concern that if they take the proverbial job in the mailroom, they will get stuck and never leave, but I've seen so many instances of upward mobility when someone was willing to be underemployed for a brief time in order to make contacts and gain industry experience," says Colorado psychologist and career counselor Dr. Janet Scarborough. So let's say you identify some grunt-job openings at companies you covet and set up some honest-to-goodness interviews. How do you ensure you're not stuck behind the front desk until the next millennium?

You and your swag

Now that you're meeting other industry pros, you need to get your shameless self-promo kit in order. People you meet at schmoozefests will want your card, not some beer-stained coaster with your number etched into it with a Swiss Army knife. Likewise, folks you ping for a brain-picking session may want to see your resume first, as my sister Naomi says, to prove "you're not the high school kid down the street." It's also a good idea to bring copies of your resume to these meetings, in case your industry insider offers to pass it along to HR. Following are some additional hints for getting your promotional package ready for public consumption:

Resume makeovers. If you have little to no experience in a particular field, revamping your resume can be a real stumper. Janet Boguch, principal of Non-Profit Works, a management consulting firm for nonprofit agencies, advises career-changers to lead their resume with a short objective statement—a sentence summing up the work you've done and the work you want to do. For example: "Pharmaceutical sales rep of five years looking to apply my deal-making prowess to a fundraising or marketing role in a nonprofit organization whose mission is to educate women about breast cancer." Next up, provide a bulleted list of three to six skills you'd bring to your new job: You're a wizard with spreadsheets, you can close a deal like nobody's business, or you can juggle seventeen tasks at once while working three phone

Audition your new boss

I'm sure you don't need me to tell you some stepping-stone gigs and the bosses they come with aren't much better than the blind date you went on when you faked a seizure so you could skip out early. So if the top dog who's interviewing you is too busy simultaneously muttering under her breath and IMing her colleagues to listen to your responses, you may want to reconsider. Ditto if your potential coworkers look one heartbeat away from checking themselves into the emergency room.

lines. Finally, launch into your chronological resume, which should include any relevant volunteer work, classes, and internships. Entire books have been devoted to the fine art of repackaging your skills and polishing your resume; for suggestions, check out the "Must-See Resources" appendix.

Digital resumes. Call me old school, but I'm not a fan of attaching your resume with the first "Hi, can I take you to coffee?" email you send someone. One computer virus is all it takes to ruin my week, so I delete all emails with attachments from people I don't know. Not only that, if you're emailing the person at work, you're likely to wind up banished to their spam folder. If showing a career hero your resume right away will help make your case for that magic coffee meeting, paste it into the text and offer to send an attachment if she prefers. Better yet, link to a simple online resume from your blog, website, or social network page and give your heroes the URL.

Business cards. If you don't have business cards, get some made, pronto. As a career-changer, you should carry them on you at all times. FedEx Kinko's and VistaPrint.com offer dirt-cheap deals. If you don't want your cards to reveal that you work in the field you're trying to ditch, provide your contact info but not your profession. Or if you're already refinishing furniture, preparing tax returns, or fixing motorcycles on the side, put that on your card.

Whether or not you're getting paid, you want to work for someone who not only is successful, sane, and personable, but will take the time—even if it's just a few minutes a week—to explain why you've been asked to spend the next month updating a computer database the size of the Milky Way. I was tasked with such a project at my last known staff job, back in the Pliocene era, while working as a publicity assistant at a New York book-publishing company. The tedium of having to research, and then call to confirm, hundreds upon hundreds of names and addresses was made more bearable (albeit only moderately so) by the knowledge that I was updating the publisher's all-important media database—the magic list of reporters the company relied on to get its books reviewed.

The idea is to sneak a peek under the hood of the business so you can learn how all the puzzle pieces fit together, not to mention how to do what the higher-ups do. Sarah, the would-be med student, who also has a knack for writing, took a summer job at a New York talent agency reading and reporting on the piles of unsolicited screenplays it received each week. Because the job was 100 percent hands on, she got to see "how the agents treat you and how they treat your script." (She chose med school. Need I say more?) And while Sarah hasn't entirely written off the scribe thing, she decided she could have a more immediate impact on the world through medicine than through the silver screen's slush pile.

To see if your job or internship will make you privy to the guts of the industry, like Sarah's did, don't be afraid to ask interviewers what you'll be doing on a daily basis and with whom (especially if the position is new), how that relates to the bigger picture of what the company does, if anyone will be training you, and whether you'll be sitting in a broom closet. Also ask what happened to the last person who had the position: Did she get promoted or run screaming for the border?

True, you can't always detect a Jekyll/Hyde situation during a forty-five-minute interview. But if you've signed up for one of those industry-specific regional discussion lists mentioned in Chapter 1, you can do some reference-checking of your own: Send a quick email to the listserv that says, "Has anyone ever worked with Widgets R Us? If so, I'd love to hear about your experiences. Please write me privately." It can help weed out the serious duds.

Get out of the mailroom - faster

Fast-forward another few weeks or months: You've accepted an internship or paid peon gig that initially seemed enviable. Only now that you've been there a while, things aren't quite so rosy. You find yourself saying, "Can I help you?" 450 times a day and living three to a bed in a studio apartment. Or maybe you're inhabiting yet another cube and doing data entry a mind-numbing four to six hours a day. Or you're holed up in some storeroom, taking inventory of printer toner and paper clips day in and day out, pining for the day when your boss gives you something—anything—more scintillating to do. It's at this juncture that you may find yourself pounding your fists on the keyboard or your head against the wall and wondering, *What the hell have I gotten myself into (again)? And how the hell do I get out?*

Take a deep breath. Even Hillary Clinton was an intern once. They call them entry-level gigs because they don't just hand out senior-management positions to people who have no idea how the heck the business works. However, there are a couple tricks to learning the ropes and climbing the ladder a little faster, and they don't involve simply keeping your head down and hoping someone takes notice of all your diligent toil.

You of course have to play nice with the other peons in the cube farm. But cozying up to the bigwigs is also key. The trick is to be sincere as if talking to a peer (rather than being a flagrant suck-up), and to offer helpful information to others (the baby sitter recommendation that salvages the boss's Friday night does the trick), rather than just being a taker.

Owning up to your successes—and failures—is critical too. Lacey Boek, who's twenty-four and works for a Pacific Northwest wine distributor, made the leap from retail clerk to sales rep in six months, rather than the two years her hiring manager told her a promotion would take. "I knew that I was qualified, but not on paper," Lacey says, "so I needed to prove to them that I have what it takes on the inside: integrity, work ethic, and drive." To make sure she stood out from the crowd, Lacey worked her tail off without complaint, often taking on extra tasks outside her job description, always treating her customers like gold. Tooting your own horn doesn't mean doing the wave every time a colleague or client pays you a compliment—the surest way to alienate your coworkers, especially the old-guard folks who already think "kids today" are a bunch of self-entitled whiners.

Yet there's nothing wrong with responding to your boss's innocuous "How's it going today?" as she breezes past with a quick, matter-of-fact comment that everything's great—in fact, you got the direct-mail project out the door a day early, which means you're free to help her work on those progress reports if she needs a hand.

I know, I know. Being chummy with the boss is all well and good when it comes time to ask for that glowing reference, but what about now, when you're the low woman on the totem pole and in grave danger of being pigeonholed as the copy-machine lackey? Susan Murphy, coauthor with Ellen Ensher of *Power Mentoring: How Successful Mentors and Protégés Get the Most out of Their Relationships,* suggests this three-step process: The next time you're in a meeting where the head honcho is fishing for bodies to help with a juicy extra-credit project that's outside your job description—perhaps putting together press kits for the upcoming product launch or creating a manual of "how we do things around here"—tell her you'd "love to help out on that." Then deliver the goods like nobody's business so the big cheese gets a glimpse of your full potential.

Your second task is to prove you're well aware there's no "I" in "team." So the *next* time the boss goes fishing for volunteers for some ultra-crappy filing or data-entry project, volunteer again. (Trust me, the silver lining's coming up.) Finally, once you've shown you can take one for the team, let someone else grab the next crap project. Instead, offer to help with one of the primo projects your boss is dishing out. In today's ridiculously overworked business world, you've got to groom yourself for the next rung on the ladder, rather than waiting for the boss to groom you.

SHOW ME THE MONEY

R emember how I told you in Chapter 1 to figure out how much you spend each month and create a budget for yourself? Well, if you didn't get to it yet, now would be a fine time to do so. Then take a look at this monthly budget, plus your research on starting salaries in your ideal new vocation, and be honest with yourself: Can you afford to make this leap tomorrow? How about in six months? How about a year from now? If you don't know yet, you're not ready to give up your day job. Erika Teschke, who spent ten years working her way up from legal secretary to supervisor, took a year to plot her escape to her new gig as a dog-walker. At thirty-six, Erika had a mortgage in Seattle and four dogs to think about. Despite having her husband's salary to help cushion the blow of her impending pay cut, she says, "The biggest thing for me—with a house and a mortgage—was working the numbers."

Besides guaranteeing she could live within her means, Erika had to ensure she had enough money saved to support the lean times. Like Erika did, you need to start saving from each paycheck—1 percent, 5 percent, 10 percent, as much as you can—and put it in a My Big Fat Career Change Fund. This is on top of any 401(k) or retirement fund you already contribute to. And cash advances on your credit cards don't count.

If you're not money savvy, get there. If your ultimate plan is to work outside the 9-to-5 realm, having a firm grip on your cash flow and savings is crucial, so you might as well start learning how it's done now. (For financial resources that can help, check out the "Must-See Resources" appendix.) Hiring a financial planner for a one-time consultation isn't a bad idea, either—even better if you have a financially responsible relative you can hit up for free advice. (My mom's counseled me on everything from paying down debt to opening an IRA to buying a home.)

If you were born in the red and money's tighter than counter space in your kitchen-slash-bedroom, now might not be the prime time for a pay cut. Transitioning into a new career—essentially, pursuing it on the side—is probably a smarter move for you, at least until you are more solvent or the side gig becomes lucrative enough to replace your current one. Chapter 3 will tell you how to stay motivated while nurturing a long-range pet project, pursuing a dream career included.

Now's also the last time in the world you want to dole out wads of cash on job-hunting accoutrements. If you need career advice or help revising your resume, tap the free resources at your disposal: your school's career center, your state's department of employment, your neighbor who works in her employer's HR department. Also, see if your local adult-education or community center offers any low-cost classes, and check your newspaper's business calendar for free or cheap lectures. If you're in school, use the free computers at the library. If you're not, use the free computers at the nearest Internet café or a friend's house. Consult a book or website for resume makeovers. Have a friend's friend who works in your dream industry read it over, and another who knows how to conjugate verbs proofread it for you. If you need help with a website, bribe a design-savvy friend with baked goods.

Some nominally priced items are, of course, worth investing in: a spiffy outfit not covered with food stains (purchased on sale or consignment) for coffee dates with your career heroes. A community college course in the computer programs or technical skills you need to flesh out your resume. Something other than a Ziploc bag to carry your business cards in.

ANTI 9-TO-5 ACTION PLAN

Another action-packed chapter! Like I said in Chapter 1, depending on how crowded your calendar is, each stage of these action plans might take you anywhere from one week to several months, sometimes even longer. Of course, the sooner you start, the sooner you can get out of your current onerous situation. So promise me you'll tackle at least one item from this plan during the next week. In fact, why don't you pick your start dates for all four stages right now, so you're not tempted to put things off? It's okay if you change some of these dates later. This just gives you a time frame to shoot for.

STAGE 1: GET YOUR SOCIAL NETWORK ON	
Start date	**Checklist**
	Create or update a profile that includes your work history on LinkedIn or another social network.
	Call your friend the resume queen to help you update your resume in exchange for a six-pack.
	Get business cards made (If you don't already have up-to-date ones).
	Update your resume or portfolio on your website or blog (if you have either).
	Select three networking events to attend in the next two months.
	Create your thirty-second face-to-face intro and practice on a couple of friends.

STAGE 2: PICK PEOPLE'S BRAINS	
Start date	**Checklist**
	Craft a short email to send to industry heroes about meeting for lunch or a coffee chat.
	Write up five or six questions to ask each of these industry insiders.
	Contact at least three people a week from your list of industry gurus (after doing some preliminary homework on them) and start setting up appointments.
	Create a folder, spreadsheet, or other nifty storage system for all your new contacts, industry notes, and job leads.

STAGE 3: **GET HANDS-ON EXPERIENCE**	
Start date	Checklist
	Arrange to volunteer at a one-time, high-profile industry event.
	If still dazzled, find yourself a steady volunteer gig in the field, even if it's just a few hours a month.
	Do your best to line up at least one or two shadowing stints with a career hero.
	Update your resume again to account for new skills, classes, and volunteer gigs.

STAGE 4: **MAKE THE LEAP**	
Start date	Checklist
	Do the math to see what type of career change you can afford, and when you can afford to make it.
	List the top five businesses or organizations in your dream career you think you want to intern or work for, and research the hell out of them.
	Begin looking for internships or starter gigs in your new field.

chapter 3

I WANT
more time to do
my
PET PROJECT
on the Side

"To begin . . . To begin . . . How to start? I'm hungry. I should get coffee. Coffee would help me think. Maybe I should write something first, then reward myself with coffee. Coffee and a muffin. So I need to establish the themes. Maybe a banana nut. That's a good muffin."

—Nicolas Cage as Charlie Kaufman in *Adaptation*, 2002

I spent the first six months of my last temp gig hating life. I'd been tasked with "webifying" marketing copy for a pressure-cooker corporate empire, and seeing as I had signed a yearlong contract, I still had six months left to go. The job—though *exciting! prestigious! a real cash cow!*—sapped most of my energy, and the onerous hourlong commute home snatched whatever shred was left. Evenings, all I wanted to do was lie on the couch as *CSI* lulled me to sleep. Weekends, I napped for nineteen hours, minimum. All the while, half-finished stories languished on my hard drive. Neglected journals collected dust on my nightstand. I ached to write, but I couldn't bear to begin. Still, I mustered up enough energy to chew myself out for letting creative atrophy take hold.

When New Year's Eve 2005 rolled around, marking the seventh month of my hellish gig, I decided it was high time I ended this pity party. In true drunken cliché form, I vowed to myself I'd start the year off, er, right. I hadn't been diagnosed with any life-threatening illness and no one I knew had died, so I couldn't chalk up my sudden conviction to one of those facing-my-mortality moments of truth. It was simply that I was sick of whining, sick of the creative void that my life had become.

And so I picked up my pen and got over my slump. I began writing in short bursts throughout the week: thirty to sixty minutes before work, on the bus ride in, in the cafeteria during lunch, in conference rooms waiting for scheduled meetings that never materialized, and on Saturday mornings before I headed out into the world with my list of errands. As you might imagine, the fog of doom and gloom soon lifted, and I tapped into energy reserves I didn't know existed. I even managed to get some of my new writing published. Besides putting a spring in my step, my rekindled love affair with all things literary made my day job less bothersome. Now that I had a life outside my bread-and-butter day gig, the bread didn't seem quite so stale.

Did I feel like I was cheating on my day gig by getting a little action on the side? A little. Did I care? Not a whit. As long as I did the work I was hired to do, delivered on time, and didn't show up a total zombie who'd been awake half the night writing, what was the harm? Besides, I'd hardly be the first woman to juggle her bread-and-butter gig with other aspirations. For years, Toni Morrison, a single mother, held down a 9-to-5 job and raised her two sons while writing bestselling novels. I probably don't need to remind you she was the first black woman to receive the Nobel Prize in Literature and the first black woman writer to hold a named chair at an Ivy League university. And Marie Curie, the mother of modern physics (and two daughters), worked on her radioactivity research while teaching physics at a girls' school. She was the first European woman awarded a PhD in research science, the first woman professor at the Sorbonne, the first woman to receive a Nobel Prize, and the first person to win a Nobel Prize in two different scientific disciplines. Nobel Prize aspirations or no, these incredibly busy women are proof that you don't need a trust fund or five years off to accomplish your goals. You just need to get started and stick with it.

Like Morrison and Curie, most of us can't afford to quit our day jobs to write award-winning literature or make world-changing scientific discoveries full-time. But that doesn't mean you have to join the ranks of the working wounded (30 percent, according to CareerBuilder.com) who say they don't have enough time to get a life outside work. If you value getting your pet project off the ground, you'll skimp on social outings, Saturday lie-ins, and anything else you can bear to sacrifice. The beauty of moonlighting is that you get to keep your paycheck while trying your hand at a new craft, social enterprise, start-up business, or career path. If your pet project turns out to be a dog, you still have a day job to fall back on.

And yes, juggling is hard, and yes, you'll be "working" much more than you were before. But you'll be working on something you *want* to do (often during the time you spent watching TV and hating your life anyway), not something your boss *told* you to do. And you'll replace all that self-loathing for neglecting your sewing, songwriting, or software programming with the thrill of finally doing it. If you're not already finding ways to fit your pet project into your daily or weekly routine, or wish you were getting your creative fix more often, this chapter will help you get on track.

IN PRAISE OF DAY JOBS

Before we go any further, I'd like to set the record straight on the so-called notion of selling out: There's no shame in having a tolerable steady gig that covers your rent, keeps you debt free, and lands you halfway decent health insurance—especially if said day gig funds your after-hours art habit or start-up idea. "I think the glamour and romance that we once assigned to being a starving artist are *so* over," says Heather Swain, who spent three years writing her first book between 5 and 7 AM before heading to work as a third grade schoolteacher. "You have to balance and compromise for art, and there's dignity in that."

In a conversation in the fall 2005 issue of *Ms.*, Kathleen Hanna, singer/guitarist in the feminist band Le Tigre, explains to 1960s bubblegum-pop legend Lesley Gore (of "It's My Party" fame) why she signed with a major label after fifteen years in the post-punk music world. As Hanna tells it, she'd had it with all the work that went into supposedly *not* selling out: booking her own shows, driving the tour van, hawking CDs from the trunk of her car, writing check after check, basically wheeling and dealing 24/7. "I thought, *Maybe I could write better songs if I wasn't on the phone all the time!*" Hanna says in the article. "So it's my feminist statement to say finally, 'I want help!'"

I realize there's a decent chance you're not an indie-rock icon with the glamorous dilemma of whether to sign with Universal Records or continue blazing the DIY trail. But when trying to nurture an after-hours project, it's hard enough to keep your stamina going without worrying about where your next paycheck is coming from. So if you already have a stable, decent-paying day job that doesn't make you stay late, commute too far, or collapse to the floor in a twitching heap, milk it for all it's worth. (If not, see "Mercenary vs. Glamour Gigs" on page 55.)

For starters, take advantage of all the business skills, computer programs, or specialized equipment (audio, video, silk-screening,

ANTI 9 to 5 tip

As tempting as it may be to go hog wild on the free color copies and office supplies at your day job, exercise restraint. Making a photocopy here and browsing a website there is no big deal, but the bigwigs won't appreciate your turning your cubicle into your home office. In other words, stay away from long-distance calls and websites that show nipple. And if making flyers for your upcoming art show or live gig, don't use all the expensive lime-green paper.

and otherwise) you could be learning on the job, perhaps as part of a company training or mentoring program. Learning how to negotiate a contract, pacify a pissed-off customer, or navigate Photoshop can come in handy for your side venture. As an added bonus, you're developing a set of skills—customer service, bookkeeping, editorial, administrative, teaching, whatever—you can fall back on later, should you need extra money (say, if you've graduated to small-business owner but need part-time or temporary work to make ends meet during a slow quarter).

But that's not all. Having to be somewhere twenty, thirty, or forty hours a week can do wonders for your creative stamina. Once you get into the groove with your pet project, you look forward to returning to it each lunch hour or weekend. But take away the structured schedule of the day job (or "fake job," as I've taken to calling mine), and most of us would piss away our weekdays catching up on our blogging or yoga classes—all well and good, unless you're still putting off that side project you'd supposedly be doing "if only you had the time." Take it from someone who knows how easy it is to waste a perfectly good afternoon on the ABC soap opera lineup.

Another case in point: When Heather left her teaching job to finish her first book (thanks to a publishing advance, some part-time tutoring work, and a supportive spouse), she had a rude awakening. Having an entire day to write didn't make her any more productive. Instead, the project expanded to fit the time available. "I learned it's not always a matter of how much time you have," she says. "When I only had that one short window, I worked my ass off." Now a mother of two with three published books under her belt, Heather's learned to get her writing done during the small chunks of time she's able to steal here and there, often when her kids are sleeping.

The moral of the story is, having more free time doesn't necessarily mean you get more done. For the discipline-impaired (present company included), more free time may just mean more hours to piddle away. As you'll see later in the chapter, sometimes the best cure for "not having enough time" isn't a free Saturday to work leisurely

Mercenary vs. glamour gigs

When it comes to finding a day job to support your side project, there are two schools of thought: those who champion mindless mercenary work and those who go for the resume-boosting, stepping-stone glamour gigs. It's hard to throw a paintbrush without hitting an aspiring artpreneur whose resume brims with barista, retail, and customer service jobs they can forget about the second their shift ends. You punch in, punch out, then go home and create. End of story. Sure, there's the danger a coworker might ask you to swap shifts with her, but there's no risk of having to pull an all-nighter to finish the big presentation to the VP of marketing.

Yet if you have kids to insure or a mortgage to pay, or you're looking for mentorship in your dream industry, you'll probably gravitate toward more of a career-track gig where you wield a clipboard, hammer, or Blackberry than your freewheeling, here-today-off-to-Ecuador-tomorrow, twenty-four-year-old, latte-making counterpart will. On the plus side, you may be making more money than you did as a supermarket cashier, and you're constantly adding those golden "marketable skills" to your growing-more-impressive-by-the-minute resume.

On the downside, there's all that pesky responsibility. That midnight cram to finalize the big "preso" to the marketing veep might rear its ugly head. If you don't mind scaling back on—or even postponing—your pet project while you learn the tricks of the trade at your glamour gig, it's no problem. But if you do, life can lose color pretty quickly. While Beena Ahmad, a former legal assistant in Manhattan, wasn't collapsing on the couch when she got off work, she did willingly put her creative writing aspirations on hold while working for a civil rights law firm that represented domestic violence victims. The never-a-dull-moment job was just too demanding, and her evenings and weekends were often usurped by day-gig writing deadlines.

If you do work in your dream industry, avoid taking a job that's too draining, requires overtime, or taps the same creative vein—writing, design, programming—you want to tap on your own time. While Beena doesn't regret a moment of her experience as a legal assistant, she's now leery of what such a demanding day gig would do to her own writing.

on your pet project—it's a bunch of thirty-minute windows in which you crank hard from the moment you sit down till the moment the clock runs out.

EXTREME TIME MANAGEMENT

Anyone who's made headway in their entrepreneurial, artsy, or social-justice side gig will tell you time is not the issue—making your project a priority is. Day gig or no, waiting for the time off, energy, or inspiration to strike before you put together your photography portfolio or start that women's self-defense center is like waiting for a couple thousand extra dollars to miraculously appear in your bank account. Think about it this way: If you were saving for a three-month trip to New Zealand, you'd cut back on takeout dinners, concert tickets, and new shoes, right? Likewise, you need to trim the fat from your non-work schedule to make room for your side gig. You also need to take your side gig as seriously as you would a hunt for a new apartment if your landlord decided to sell the building out from under you. Sacrificing sleep, meals, and exercise doesn't count. Nixing reality TV and long, meandering emails to your friends about your latest dating crisis does. Like Mom used to say, life is about making choices.

You don't have to nix all your downtime—you don't want to burn out or become a hermit. Just see where you can scale back, if only by an hour or two a week. To see where your biggest time hits are, take a written inventory of how you spend your non-working hours for a week or two, a little exercise I call Timesuck Target Practice. If you're anything like me, you'll discover you spend untold hours instant-messaging friends, rearranging your closet, and reading online personal ads you have no intention of answering—time you could devote to something a tad more productive.

Instead of meeting friends two nights a week, cut back to one. If you live with a partner or children, you'll have to be that much more vigilant about "me" time. Usually, this will involve hiding in a back room with an ENTER AND I'LL SHOOT! sign, escaping to a café, or relying heavily on your kid's sleeping patterns. It should not involve neglecting to feed your offspring or pretending your domestic partner has inexplicably vaporized.

Even if you're less frivolous than me, chances are you spend an hour or two a week waiting for something or someone—like the subway or a friend who's late for dinner. If you drive to work (or crawl there, as is standard practice in Seattle), bring along a tape recorder to brainstorm ideas. Better still, ditch your car keys, grab a pen and paper, and hop on the bus. Look for unlikely places to work on your side project, like in your doctor's waiting room or on the post office line. Scribbling in your notebook in the Laundromat certainly beats reading the takeout menus and three-year-old issues of *Guns & Ammo* they have lying around.

ANTI 9 to 5 tip

According to a recent Salary.com survey, the average cube-dweller admits to wasting two hours of each eight-hour workday (excluding lunch). Sound familiar? When making your own Timesuck Target Practice list, don't overlook all the hours you fritter away on the job—Googling exes, playing online Texas Holdem, cruising the halls for homemade fudge. As Janet Rosen, a New York stand-up comic who doubles as a literary agent, suggests, when you're at your day gig, pretend "the taxi meter is on." In other words, learn to focus and compartmentalize. The faster you get in and out of your place of employ, the more time you'll have for the work you really want to do.

Bite-size pieces

If you're having trouble making the leap from burned-out wage slave to dedicated artpreneur, it's possible your ambitions are so lofty (overnight millionaire, NEA grant recipient, the next Gloria Steinem), you don't know where to begin. Or maybe—to further psychoanalyze you—you're too busy playing the comparison game, poring over the websites of successful businesswomen, activists, and artists. But instead of drawing inspiration, you give up before you even start. All this creative angst is about as productive as expecting to sprout gigantic biceps your first week at the gym. You've got to start somewhere, just like your creative idols did (no doubt while couch-surfing or toiling away at a day job). And taking small bites is the quickest route to success.

In her book *Bird by Bird: Some Instructions on Writing and Life*—devoured by everyone from schoolteachers to musicians in my circle of friends—author Anne Lamott suggests those having trouble sitting their asses in the writing chair task themselves with cranking out just enough lines of text to be visible through "a one-inch picture frame," an act that takes all of a few minutes. The book goes on to offer, among other gems, the liberating advice to write "shitty first drafts." At least you're beginning to tackle the project, which, any instructor or career coach will tell you, is the hardest part. You can always revise your business plan, webpage design, or any other plans for world domination later.

But it's not enough to make a Timesuck Target Practice list, identify a few hours a week to devote to your side project, and tell yourself you'll fill a few picture frames. You have to crack open your day planner and block off some non-negotiable time slots to devote to your side gig *each week,* just as you would a doctor's appointment or dinner date. Call them something fun, like Weapons of Mass Construction (or WMC). Start with super-small chunks at least two or three times a week, and not just on weekends—for example, you might block off 7 to 7:30 AM before work on Wednesdays and Fridays, and 1 to 1:30 PM on Sundays. Don't tackle a four-hour session right out of the gate; one hour or less is infinitely easier to stick to.

The more frequent your WMC sessions, the more you'll look forward to the next one. The idea is to get hooked, as hooked as you are on your morning coffee or evening run with the dog. Use a wall calendar, notebook, or spreadsheet to measure your progress: how much time you spent on your project each session and what you accomplished. This will help you see the bigger picture come into focus. "All the little things and the hard work do add up. You just might not notice them right away," says Sarah Varon, who divides her time between freelance illustration for publications like *The New York Times*, the graphic novels she pens, and a part-time job in the printmaking department of a New York arts college.

If you're having the work week from hell or your in-laws come to town for a visit, cut yourself some slack. The world won't end if you skip a couple of WMC sessions to catch up on sleep or restock your fridge. Do try to touch your pet project every week, though, even if you just research real estate investment properties during your lunch hour, brainstorm business logos on the commute home, or thumb through a craft magazine before falling asleep. The longer you stay away from your side gig, the harder it is to get back into it. And the more you look at other people's ideas and art, the more it feeds your own imagination.

ANTI 9 to 5 tip

One trick many writers use to help stoke the "I can't wait to get back to what I'm working on" fire is stopping midsentence. Whether you work in stitches, brushstrokes, or HTML, try it. Ten bucks says you'll have an easier time planting your butt in the chair when your next WMC session rolls around.

Morning glory or Elvira?

The shortest path to addiction is to develop a routine. You may have to try a variety of time slots before you land on a side-gig schedule that works best for you. I'd never thought of myself as one of those people who's insanely chipper at the crack of dawn, but I quickly learned that getting any writing done after a full day's toil at a 9-to-5 contract gig was a lost cause. I was too fried. So I learned to relish—okay, tolerate—rising before dawn to write on days designated in my calendar as "WMC hunt."

If waking before the birds sounds positively draconian to you, you have other options. Go in to work a half-hour early a couple times a week. Something about being at a desk makes even the biggest vampires snap to. Plus, the coffee's free. Or eat at your desk and then use your lunch hour for a midday creativity snack: Pick the brain of an entrepreneurial hero, score a web deal on a luscious vintage fabric, or make some calls for that reproductive-rights fundraiser you're putting together.

If you can't squeeze one more minute out of the daylight hours, there are a few tricks for giving yourself a 6, 7, or 8 PM pick-me-up (besides a brisk walk or a sweaty yoga class) so you can squeeze in a WMC session. A change of scenery after a hard day's drudgery can give you that much-needed creative shot in the arm. Find a café couch, library table, or barstool of your own and get to work. Or stop somewhere that inspires you before heading home, be it a gorgeous building by an architect you admire, the business section of your favorite bookstore, or the window of an art gallery. If working on your craft at home during evenings, crib a page from Janet, the comic/literary agent: Grab a light snack and do the deed *before* sitting down to dinner. After a full meal, you're twice as likely to blow off anything you'd been planning to do when you walked in the door.

If you're at your desk or easel but having trouble getting started, Keri Smith, author of *Living Out Loud: Activities to Fuel a Creative Life*, suggests doodling, journaling, blogging, playing scales, or otherwise noodling for five to ten minutes to jump-start your right brain. Just use this exercise as a warm-up, like stretching before a run, rather than as a substitute for the work you really want to do.

Switching projects can help, too. Sometimes you have to play tricks on your mind to make it cooperate (*Ha ha! I'm getting away with not doing the thing I said I would do after work!*). If you start building webpage B instead of finishing webpage A, it still counts as web design—as long as you don't wind up with six months' worth of unfinished pages. If you find yourself endlessly noodling or stalling, it could be that you're afraid to finish. Because the next step after finishing is showing your masterpiece to others, and, well, what if they hate it? Just remind yourself that when it comes to giving feedback, most people are about 900 times kinder than scathing *American Idol* judge Simon Cowell, and a little constructive criticism never killed anyone. If anything, it will make you better at what you do.

GET A ROOM

Between your calendar appointments and snowballing side-gig obsession, you should be well on your way to resisting the allure of the TV remote. Still, a particularly mind-numbing day in the cube or on your feet might make you extra susceptible to what I like to think of as The Couch Factor, the inertia that binds one's derriere to the sofa like a tongue to a frozen flagpole. That's when it's time to make Virginia Woolf proud and go to your room.

You need a comfortable, quiet, distraction-proof spot to work on your side gig—a place in the house designated as yours and yours alone. Alcoves, walk-in closets, basements, garages, workshops, and spare bedrooms are great choices. If you live in a shoebox where square footage is in short supply, or in a home crammed with preschool toys, you might need to get creative. Personally, I'm a big fan of the kitchen table and bedroom corner.

Proven procrastination-busters

If you've ever glanced at your computer, saxophone, or sewing machine, only to be overcome by an inexplicable urge to mop the floor or alphabetize your CD collection, there's a good chance you suffer from the nasty p-word. For additional tips on how to get down to business, I consulted some of the world's most notorious procrastinators: a bunch of professional writers I know (names are withheld to protect the guilty). Here's what they suggest:

Unplug. Devices that beep, ding, ring, or air *Law and Order* reruns nonstop are the enemy. Don't just turn down the sound—shut off the phone, modem, and tube altogether. Every minute you're reading the headlines or texting a friend about the softball-size hail outside is a minute you're not working on your project. While you're at it, remove Solitaire, Mah-Jongg, and any other games from your computer. I've even gone so far as to cancel my cable TV and e-newsletter subscriptions.

Pop in a CD. This one reminds me of my marathon road trip days. To get through the home stretch, I'd guzzle some caffeine, crank up the stereo, and drive till I crossed the state line. Try it: Turn up your favorite CD and get to work on that golden project until the last track fades out. If you can't work to music, set an alarm for an hour. Caffeine optional.

Swab the decks. You really want to mop the floor instead of working on that comic book you've been meaning to finish for the past five years? Fine. Start scrubbing—but only for fifteen minutes. One of two things will probably happen: You'll mop for fifteen minutes, your mind will start racing, and you'll get excited to dive back into your project. Or you'll drop the mop, rush to your computer (or camera or easel), and start working immediately. Depends on how much you hate to clean.

If after six months your habit has developed into a full-blown addiction and you have the cash and inclination to rent a humble workspace outside your home, go for it. Renting your own affordable—albeit tiny—desk space, art studio, or band practice spot is easier than you might think. (Just don't go for broke. If you're planning to go solo or cut back on your hours at your bread-and-butter gig anytime soon, you'll need all the spare cash you can save).

Reward thyself. I used to live with a would-be screenwriter who'd work for fifty minutes of every hour, then reward himself with the next ten minutes of whatever *Star Wars or Star Trek* movie he was in the midst of watching. Total nerdfest, right? But this delayed-gratification game works for many creative types and small-business owners I know (though not all of them go for sci-fi flicks). Work on your project for a set period of time, then make a sundae or surf the web—but only if you put in the time first.

Never mind Pulitzer quality. Maybe you're putting too much pressure on yourself to be brilliant, perfect, prodigylike. Your creations don't have to be *War and Peace.* In fact, perfect isn't really an attainable goal, since we're all flawed in our own charming ways. Wouldn't "really fucking great" work just as well? Give yourself permission to lower the bar a little.

Hit rock bottom. If you find yourself clasping your hands with glee and exclaiming, "Oh, is *The OC* on tonight? I have to see who Ryan's screwing this week!" fine, do it. Watch two hours of trash TV while you're at it. Watch until you're so disgusted with yourself that you race to your desk afterward (or the next morning, when you wake up with an imprint of the couch cushions on your face) to wash the bad taste out of your mouth.

If you're having trouble hanging in there for an entire hour, break the task down further into thirty- or fifteen-minute increments. Use an egg timer if you have to. Seriously. It works. Then repeat until you've used up the hour. Try to remember that you *like* doing whatever it is you're forcing yourself to do. Whenever I feel myself getting cranky about sitting down to write, I remind myself that I could just go out and get a 9-to-5 job instead. That usually puts an end to my griping pretty quick.

Many cities are home to warehouses converted into dozens, if not hundreds, of nominally priced, rentable workspaces. On the West Coast, for example, ActivSpace has transformed nine warehouse-style buildings into clean, safe, quiet studios moonlighters and business owners can rent on a month-to-month basis. In Brooklyn, the Office-Ops arts and event center rents out reasonably priced studios, practice space, and media equipment rooms. To find the good workspaces in your hood, check with your local chamber of commerce and arts commission. Also check websites like ArtistHelpNetwork.com and that digital hub of all things rentable—craigslist.

THE BUDDY SYSTEM

There's nothing like someone else's boot marks on your ass—be they those of an instructor or a like-minded side-gigger—as incentive to get serious about your pet project. One surefire way to keep your brain churning after hours is to take night classes. The structure helps prod you along, as does the fact that you've coughed up cold hard cash to be there. And nothing shames you into productivity like a weekly homework assignment. Beena, the former legal assistant, proved this when she joined a women's writing workshop during her second year on the job; thanks to the workshop deadlines, she wrote a new story every couple of months.

More important, connecting with other members of your creative tribe is a must. Suddenly, you're not the lone freak in the cube who dreams of building a dog sweater–knitting empire; you're one of fifteen people at a stitch 'n' bitch with similar aspirations. As someone who's worked solo since the Clinton administration (ah, the good old days), I've tried more ways than I care to admit, most of them free, to stay on track and get that much-needed camaraderie. Some favorites follow.

Contests and grants. Submitting your art for publication or display, entering a contest, or applying for an artist's grant or fellowship gives you a firm deadline to work toward. If you don't turn in your submission or application, you don't get published, shown, or awarded. Yes, there's a decent chance you'll get a rejection letter, but you'll still get the work done, which is the main goal. Many writers and artists I know—including me—planted the first seeds of their creative habit by working to these external deadlines. Renting a table at a craft fair or flea market, or splitting a trade-show booth with a couple of small-business owners, can yield the same results.

Brainstorming groups. This is like the Diva Night concept from Chapter 2, only with a more formal agenda. Invite four to eight women you know with similar side gigs or aspirations—other social-preneurs, green thumbs, or business-tycoons-in-training. Meet every four to six weeks to troubleshoot each other's burning enterprise issues and share success stories. Potlucks in homes or corner tables in quiet cafés work well. Have one person facilitate each meeting to keep the conversation on topic and ensure everyone gets their turn to talk. Steer clear of wannabes with far less experience than you; you'll get more out of the group if the other photographers in it already have some experience dealing with magazine editors, commercial clients, or stock photo agencies. Make the group invite-only. If the other members are as dedicated as you to their side projects, they'll appreciate the exclusivity. You want a group of active, supportive contributors, not ravenous rookies who hang on your every word (that's what's known as teaching).

Workout partners. Having a creative-workout partner is a lot like having a gym or cycling buddy. No matter what the activity, you and your partner give each other the boot in the butt on a regular basis, even if you're not "working out" in each other's presence. When I work with a writing buddy (in our own homes, on our own schedules), here's what we do: Each Monday morning, we swap writing schedules and goals over email. If we feel like touching base during the week, we email each other a short note saying something like, "I'm kicking ass! Woohoo!" or, "I'm dying over here. Can you talk me off the ledge?" On Sunday nights, we have a short phone chat about how much we wrote, where we came up short, and why. Basically, we cheer each other on and dole out the tough love as needed.

Collaborators. My friend Annie, a filmmaker and photographer who spends her days freelancing as an event producer in the high-tech world, kicks the workout-buddy concept up a notch by collaborating with other creative types. Sometimes she'll write a screenplay or shoot a short film with a partner. Other times she'll take photos to accompany a writer pal's prose. The collective deadline keeps all involved parties honest. "You both want to finish the project and you're both invested in it, so it's not just you who's let down if you drop the ball," she says.

ANTI 9 to 5 tip

To find like-minded enterprising women in your neck of the woods, see the bulletin boards in your favorite cafés, stores, and community centers. Also check out online discussion forums and lists offered on sites like MediaBistro.com, Craftster.org, DigitalEve .org, and those countless Meetup.com and Yahoo! groups.

SHOW ME THE MONEY

If you've already put a moratorium on shoe spending and kicked the latte factor, congrats on your downsizing efforts. But don't stop there. When securing supplies and services for your side gig, try bartering with friends or local businesses. Michelle Madhok, owner of SheFinds.com, is the perfect example of a barter-happy businesswoman. Because her office is inundated with swag from companies hoping to get listed on her site, she trades boxes of beauty products for ad space. While you may not have freebies to give out like candy, as Michelle does, perhaps you have a business or domestic skill or a product you can offer as currency. For instance, if you're trying to build up a landscape design business on the side, like my friend

Maria, you could trade a free back yard consultation with a graphic artist in exchange for her creating your logo. Be sure to trade hours rather than tasks, and put an expiration date on the trade so everyone's happy.

Buy your office and craft supplies wholesale or in bulk, even if you won't be using or selling them right away. "In the long run, it's cheaper to spend a little bit of money to get things wholesale," says Maggie Kleinpeter, who's well versed in buying blank T-shirts by the dozen for her silk-screening business. The web and Costco can help here, and you may want to divvy up bulk buys with an artpreneur pal to save cash. But avoid whipping out your wallet before making a prototype and testing the market for your side venture. I still have $500 worth of unused beads I bought a million years ago, back when I thought I was going to start my own earring-making enterprise. Little did I know you had to actually make the earrings in order for anyone to buy them.

Also check estate sales, eBay, thrift shops, and—if you work at a big company—the classifieds at your office. And don't overlook the freebies on Freecycle.org. Take full advantage of your local library, too, and if you must own reference books, visit used bookstores and discount websites like AbeBooks.com. And next time your mom asks what you want for your birthday, tell her you want a subscription to *Practical Welding Today* or whatever publication you've been coveting. Whenever possible, rent or borrow equipment like power tools and digital scanners. Now is not the time to take out a loan or max out your credit cards. Remember, baby steps. (We'll talk about funding a business or nonprofit organization in Part II of the book.)

For artist's grants or residencies, check with your city or state arts commission for a list of local grants and foundations. Also check with ArtistCommunities.org. Know that the competition will be stiff and you may not get immediate results, especially if your portfolio is in its infancy. Before you apply, attend any orientations the foundations you're interested in offer. If you can, ask for tips from others who've applied.

ANTI 9-TO-5 ACTION PLAN

R eady to roll up your sleeves and start making moonlighting a reality? These steps will send you on your way.

STAGE 1: PUT ON YOUR BATHING CAP	
Start date	**Checklist**
	Make your Timesuck Target Practice list to track where the hours go each week.
	Buy, barter for, or borrow the tools you need to work on your side gig: computer, office supplies, power tools, art gear, whatever.
	Get a book or magazine related to your project and thumb through it. Inspiring!

STAGE 2: WADE IN	
Start date	**Checklist**
	Use your Timesuck Target Practice list to carve out at least one to three hours a week for your project. If you have a partner and kids, tell them about your goals.
	In your weekly calendar, block out at least two time slots to work on your project. Find a place to work uninterrupted. Let family know this is your "office," even if it's the linen closet.
	Start creating, building, or scheming, and track your progress— how long you worked and what you accomplished.

STAGE 3: START DOG-PADDLING	
Start date	Checklist
	Begin to set small, manageable creative goals: Write a snippet of computer code each WMC session, touch up three pictures in Photoshop, or set up two informational interviews.
	Vary when and where you work to see what's most productive for you (or when your kids sleep soundest). If working after hours, try a couple of the evening pick-me-ups on page 60.
	If it's discipline you need, try two or three of the procrastination-busters on page 62.

STAGE 4: LOSE THE KICKBOARD AND FLOATIES	
Start date	Checklist
	Gauge your momentum. If you're only working on your side gig an hour or two a week, see if you can step it up by another hour or two.
	Take steps to meet creative buddies you can brainstorm or set goals with.
	Milk your day job for all it's worth: Resolve to learn—on the company's dime—one new business skill, program, or piece of equipment every month or two.

Part II
FLEE the CUBE

chapter 4

I want a more FLEXIBLE work schedule

"I can't keep working like this. I'm going to have to cut back to fifty hours a week—fifty-five, tops."

—Cynthia Nixon as Miranda Hobbes on *Sex and the City*

Lynn Finnel is this über-mountaineer I met a few years ago at one of my temp gigs in the wonderful world of software programming. While my coworkers and I would spend our summer weekends cooking up bratwursts, swilling beer, and lounging about our back yards, Lynn, who's forty-eight, would be out scaling some 10,000-foot peak or other. One Monday she came to work limping. Apparently she'd sprained her ankle on Mount Hood (11,249 feet), taped it, popped some ibuprofen, and drove her stick shift 100 miles or so to meet friends for a hike up Mount St. Helens (8,364 feet). So it came as no surprise when Lynn told me she'd gone from forty to thirty hours a week at her day job so she could devote more time her dream gig, working as a volunteer climbing ranger on Washington's Mount Rainier.

Going part-time has made a mountain of difference for Lynn. A former community college professor, she began working in high-tech in 1999 because her mortgage beckoned and she needed a more solid income. (Prior to her professor gig, Lynn taught ESL in Seoul and worked as a machinist at an aircraft manufacturer, among other adventures.) Before scaling back her hours at her project management job, she worked two or three weekends a month on Rainier, patrolling the mountain, giving climbers weather and route information, and helping with search-and-rescue operations. But it was a grueling schedule that had Lynn going straight from work Friday afternoons to the peak, which is two and a half hours away, and returning to her office gig the following Monday morning. And because she had to get up to a 10,000-foot-altitude base camp Friday nights to make the most of each weekend, she scarcely had enough time to acclimate to the altitude change.

These days, Lynn cuts out of her day gig early on Thursdays and spends an extra three days a month on Rainier. It's a schizophrenic life: On Monday mornings, after three straight days of braving the elements and saving lives, the librarylike setting of her corporate gig—and the fact that all her coworkers bathe on a daily basis—takes some getting used to. "Once, I actually had to remind myself not to go to the bathroom outside," she says. But since Lynn can't pay her mortgage being a seasonal mountain ranger, juggling the two jobs is the next best thing.

If you're reading this chapter, there's a decent chance you're among the 50 percent of U.S. workers who say that, like Lynn, they'd happily take a pay cut in exchange for more time off work. Even if you're not up for the pay cut, there's a good chance you can relate to the 67 percent of Gen X women who in 2005 told Catalyst, a leading research group on women's career advancement, that they want a compressed work week, or the 59 percent of them who said they wanted to telecommute. Maybe you want the extra time to devote to your one true vocational love—be it mountain rescue, event planning, or tap dancing. Maybe you could use an extra day a week to sow the seeds of your upstart landscaping business. Or maybe you'd do anything to be home when your kids get out of school.

Whatever the reason, this chapter will discuss several ways you can trade in your rigid 9-to-5 schedule for a more flexible one. This might mean crunching numbers all day as a CPA while learning to bartend at night, or trading in your full-time gig for two less demanding part-time ones. Cutting back your work hours altogether, like Lynn did, is another solution. But for those who can't afford to work less than forty hours a week, telecommuting, flextime, or contract work may be a better bet. This chapter will give you the skinny on all these options. So let's get this flex-work party started, shall we?

Does your day gig need a makeover?

Determining if your day gig is getting in the way of the rest of your life isn't brain surgery. And by "getting in the way," I mean preventing you from having any hobbies, side projects, social life, or quality time with your family—or preventing you from sleeping if you *do* choose to embrace life outside work. To make this call, check any of the following statements that ring true:

❏ Between your day gig and your side project, you're working sixty to eighty hours a week (or more).

❏ You don't remember what your eyes look like without the bags that invariably accompany them.

❏ You haven't had a day off since the Clinton administration.

❏ Your work at your day gig is suffering because you've been up till 3 AM with your side project every night this week.

❏ You're so stressed out, you accidentally flipped off the HR director while pulling out of the company parking lot.

❏ Your kids haven't seen you in so long, they start to cry when "the strange lady who just walked in the door" kisses them hello.

❏ Your partner hasn't seen you in so long, s/he filed a missing persons report.

If you checked any of these statements, something's got to give. And since you're not likely to give up your art obsession, side business, or family, you may want to think about giving your day gig a face-lift. I'm not just talking about wallpapering your cube with tinfoil or color copies of your pet Labradoodle. I'm talking a change in job description, schedule, and perhaps even employer. The rest of this chapter will give you some ideas.

THE JOY OF FLEX

Besides going part-time, flex work can mean shuffling when and where you clock your forty hours a week. Following are the mainstays of flex-work setups.

Flextime. One of the reasons I took my last temp gig was that I knew the company supported flexible work hours. The cast of characters I worked with was a potpourri of flexies: Andrea, the cosmetology school student you met in Chapter 1, worked as a web producer from 7 or 8 AM till 4 PM so she could make it to her 5 PM classes in time. Roz, the weekend entrepreneur, crammed her forty-hour work week as a product manager into four ten-hour days so she'd have Fridays off to grow her home-based retail business. And since I'm not much for making eye contact before noon, I usually rolled in around 10 AM, unless—blast it!—I had an early-morning meeting.

Split shift. This is pretty much a variation of the traditional flextime setup. A mother of three I sat next to at that same temp gig often worked mornings at the office and evenings at home, after her kids went to bed. And Katherine Batey, one of my local bus drivers, splits her weekday gig between two four-hour shifts, one in the morning, one in the evening. Having afternoons off to kick back is pretty blissful for this midlifer, especially after years of raising kids and holding down stressful office jobs.

Telecommuting. For Amanda Kelly, thirty-seven, an independent communications pro and a divorced mom with five kids, telecommuting is a serious time and sanity saver. Besides saving a small fortune in gas, telecommuters get the same amount of work done in about three-quarters the time it takes their meeting-saturated counterparts. But working from home isn't just a luxury of the self-employed. Ann Wolken, thirty-four, finagled telecommuting two days a week for her graphic-design job at the University of Washington. And although attorney Lisa Herb, thirty-nine, lives in New York, she works from home for several Seattle firms on a contract basis. She also recently spent eighteen months telecommuting from Mongolia because her wildlife biologist husband had a too-good-to-pass-up job offer there.

Job sharing. If you saw the movie *Nine to Five,* you've seen job sharing in action (that is, after Lily, Jane, and Dolly tie up their boss and start dispensing flex-work arrangements like candy, thrilling the moms on staff who need to leave early to pick up their kids after school). Mandy Beck, who works as a book editor, negotiated one of these prized work arrangements when her company was downsizing. She and another mom who wanted more quality time with the kids split a full-time position 50/50.

Freelancing. Ah, the wonderful world of self-employment. As you probably know, a freelancer provides a creative, professional, or other type of service to individuals and companies. Sometimes referred to as independent contractors, free agents, sole proprietors, small-business owners, and—depending on whom you ask—slackers, we freelancers get to call the shots on everything from our schedules to our projects to our hourly rate. On the flip side, we don't get paid sick days, and, well, sometimes being the boss can be a real bitch. More on working solo in the next two chapters.

Temping or contracting. There's no shame in being a short-timer. For those who don't want to commit to one employer, maybe because they're planning to launch a business, pen their memoirs, or buy a one-way ticket to Timbuktu as soon as they save enough cash, working as a temp or contractor can be a great option.

Temp gigs have come a long way since the Kelly Girls of the sixties, when women began working as temporary clerks, typists, and secretaries in droves. Though today's temp and contract gigs are most abundant for techies, creative types, and anyone with a shred of office skills, staffing agencies recruit bodies for teaching, housekeeping, nursing, jackhammering, truck driving, and umpteen other vocations. Assignments can last a week, a season, even a year or more. According to the American Staffing Association, the average stint is three to five months.

When I need to pay off a huge heap of bills or save for a big purchase, taking a several-month contract to work as a copywriter or web editor at some corporate office—cubicle and all—is my medicine of choice. Because the work is steady and my overhead is zero, I earn more as a permatemp than I normally do as a freelancer. (Otherwise, don't you think I'd be home, working in my skivvies?) What's more, if you're more of an industry newbie, temping is a fantastic way to test-drive a company you're curious about and wedge your foot in the door. For more on temping and contracting, see the "Temp Survival Guide" appendix.

Late shift. Bartenders and restaurant workers don't hold the monopoly on late shifts and evening work. Seattle massage therapist Lesley Ernst, thirty-seven, works from 1 to 8 pm four days a week so she can spend mornings with her three-year-old daughter. Her carpenter husband gets off work at three-thirty, at which time he picks up their little one from daycare and goes on dad duty. And when Christine Gebhart's naval officer husband was stationed outside the United

ANTI 9 to 5 *tip*

Before you go monkeying with your work schedule, talk to your boss about the fact that you're overworked—especially if you were hired to work forty hours a week but are regularly putting in fifty-five. Ask your manager for a lighter workload, fewer keep-you-awake-at-night responsibilities, or help from your coworkers. Of course, if the company culture dictates that employees put in twelve hours on a "slow" workday, you have some bigger career decisions to make.

States, the forty-year-old worked from three-thirty to midnight as a shipyard electrician in Washington so she had more daylight hours with her teenage son.

NOT ALL JOBS ARE CREATED FLEXIBLE

A lthough it's hard to pick up the Sunday business section of your favorite newspaper without stumbling upon an article about the never-ending quest for work/life balance, flex jobs remain the exception, not the rule. The good news is, more and more U.S. companies are wising up to the fact that people who aren't tearing their hair out from stress make more productive, loyal employees. "The smarter employers have figured out it's in their self-interest and helps their bottom line," says Cindia Cameron, organizing director of 9to5, National Association of Working Women.

In 2006, the U.S. Chamber of Commerce reported that 27.5 percent of workers have flextime and 17 percent have part-time jobs. So where are all these coveted flex jobs? Some are in Fortune 500 corporations. Others are in the mom-and-pop venture down the street from you. In fact, a 2005 study by the Families and Work Institute showed that companies with less than 100 employees are more likely to embrace flexible work options.

Obviously, some industries are more conducive to flex schedules than others. It's easier to walk into that cute little art gallery downtown or nonprofit community center with aspirations of working from 11 AM to 6 PM and telecommuting one day a week than it is if you're interviewing for a position as a bank teller.

But arts and nonprofit organizations don't hold a monopoly on flex gigs that give you more leeway to pursue those side projects near and dear to you. Jobs in the media, creative services, and high-tech sectors are notorious for their alternative schedules and openness to telecommuting. Alternative healthcare gigs—massage therapist, acupuncturist, yoga instructor—also lend themselves more easily to flex schedules, given that they're appointment based and found in environments where Enya usually runs on a continuous loop. Ditto for home repairwomen and service providers like pet sitters and housekeepers. Moral of the story: If a flexible schedule is a priority for you, get yourself trained in a field that doesn't require you to occupy a seat at corporate HQ eight to ten hours every day.

ODE TO THE PATCHWORK PAYCHECK

The more years I spend hunched over a keyboard in the most sedentary job known to womankind, the more I fantasize about getting a part-time gig that lets me move my rear a little—shoveling dirt, picking up dog poop, whatever—as long as it gets the blood pumping and gives me a breather from stringing sentences together.

I certainly wouldn't be the only woman to embrace the patchwork paycheck. Janet Rosen, the New York literary agent and stand-up comic you met in Chapter 3, considers both jobs her dream gig. Seattleite Krystal Perkins, twenty-eight, also thrives on having more than one gig. The mother of two splits her work week between her job as a real estate agent and the real estate staging business that she co-owns with a friend. "I'm a little ADD in the fact that I always have to be working on something," Krystal says. The busier she is, the happier she is.

And Mistress Blue, thirty-four, a dominatrix who's been in business since 2001, says her role-playing work is too draining to do eight hours a day. Providing "erotic domination and fetish services for a fee" four hours a day is about all she can handle. (In case you're as curious as I was about what these services entail, she explains that "sometimes they involve pain, sometimes they involve bondage, a lot of times they involve dress-up.") Besides the psychic drain of doing this work, there are all those costume changes to think about. So instead of donning leather and stilettos full-time, Mistress Blue doubles as a freelance writer for a bondage site, with her dom work commanding 60 to 70 percent of her overall income.

For countless artpreneurs, the patchwork paycheck is a happy medium between wage slavedom and total self-employment. "I learned to love the part-time gig because waiting for the freelance check to come is such a pain in the ass," says New York writer and dating advice columnist Judy McGuire. And Sara Varon, the graphic novelist you met in Chapter 3, finds balancing a menagerie of part-time work much breezier than dealing with the monotony and brain drain of a steady 9-to-5 gig.

"It's that idea of wearing multiple hats," says *Kiss Off Corporate America* author Lisa Kivirist. "People ask you to tell them what you do for a living, and you say, 'Take a seat.'" Multiple hats mean multiple sources of income. If you lose one job, you're not 100 percent unemployed in an instant—you still have your other work to fall back on. When you know you can pick up some stopgap work tending bar, snapping wedding photos, or writing resumes, you're less inclined to obsess about money.

KNOW WHAT YOU STAND TO LOSE

Different people are comfortable making different concessions. Call me a commitment-phobe, but I'm far more freaked by the idea of showing up to the same office every day than I am by not collecting a steady paycheck. I didn't always used to be this way. But the more I work for myself, the more I relish the variety of juggling a multitude of projects for a multitude of clients, not to mention the freedom of working from home. I have friends who are polar opposites, though: All the Paxil in the world couldn't quell their panic over leaving the 9-to-5 nest for a more flexible, autonomous career.

If you're considering flex work, I assume you're willing to make some career trade-offs to get a life outside the office. But before you type up your request for flex, give some serious thought to what you stand to lose financially and status-wise by swapping your traditional

9-to-5 for a part-time, temp, or telecommuting gig. Some companies may agree to a flex arrangement in one breath, then ship you off to career Siberia in the next, slashing your salary, benefits, and even your promotability.

"Being part-time is not supposed to hurt your career opportunities, but I think it has to," says Lynn, the high-tech worker and volunteer mountain-climbing ranger, "because if you go part-time, it means you have other things you'd rather do with your life, be it kids or side interests."

Lynn's not alone in this belief. In a 2005 Catalyst study, 68 percent of Gen X women said that they think commitments to personal or family responsibilities prevent women from advancing at work (curiously, only 38 percent of their male counterparts agreed with this statement). In other words, the mommy track isn't just for moms anymore, it's for anyone who picks quality of life over wage slavedom. Herewith some of the worst offenses of today's work/ life balance programs.

That pesky wage gap

If you think earning 77 cents to every man's dollar stinks, get a load of the part-time wage gap, in which part-time workers often make less per hour than their full-time counterparts. "Unfortunately, part time positions in this country usually come with a pay cut and few, if any, benefits," write Joan Blades and Kristin Rowe-Fink beiner, authors of *The Motherhood Manifesto: What America's Moms Want—And What to Do About It.* According to 9to5, National Association of Working Women, 72 percent of part-time workers are women, and going part-time means taking a 40 percent pay cut.

The ideal, of course, is to retain a prorated version of your salary (and as many bennies as you can) when you go part-time. So if you're going from forty hours a week to thirty, you shouldn't incur more than a 25 percent pay cut. For help talking dollars with your current boss or a potential new one, see "No-Fear Negotiation" in the appendix.

If you do manage to keep your prorated salary after dropping your hours, beware of scope creep—the ever-growing workload that no human (no matter how caffeinated) could complete in a part-time work week. A few women I talked to who transitioned to part-time said their managers continue to pile a full-time workload on their plate, meaning they're getting paid less to do the same job as before. According to *The Motherhood Manifesto*, this is a common issue for part-timers.

Who ate my benefits?

Though no full-time gig is forever (downsizing, anyone?), you'll have an easier time nabbing that golden health coverage as a full-timer. A recent report from the Sloan Work and Family Research Network shows that 81 percent of part-time workers don't have any health benefits to speak of. Of course, I didn't have any trouble tracking down part-timers working at mega-corporations, creative agencies, media firms, universities, and nonprofit organizations who get free or partially subsidized health insurance through their jobs. But as the authors of *The Motherhood Manifesto* point out, the more highly skilled you are, the better your flex-work options.

Some benefits may be harder to acquire as a part-timer: paid leave, retirement plan, and paid tuition, to name a few. As for job-hopping temps like me, we consider ourselves lucky if we get even a partially subsidized health plan. And though a few temp agencies have offered me a retirement plan, I've never stuck around the five years required to see the dang thing vest (meaning, I could have put the money in any old retirement account; I didn't need the temp agency's help to do it).

I realize this is getting into all sorts of logistics you were probably hoping to avoid when you first thought to flee the cube, but like I've been saying, getting your money straight is part of plotting your escape plan. Sometimes flex jobs are the best way to fit in and fund a new freelance career or business venture, even if they're just stepping-stones along the way to self-employment or doing the work you dream of.

I don't get no respect

If you're like Kim Rush, forty-two, who's already spent umpteen years toiling for the Man and, since the unexpected death of her brother, has come to value face time with family far more than face time at the office, what I'm about to say probably won't matter to you. Even if you haven't toiled for the Man much, what I'm about to say may not matter to you. (It certainly never did to me.)

Kim, a Seattle mother of two, recently landed a plum part-time gig directing a creative studio, partly because she first spent a decade working her way up the ranks at a ginormous corporation. If you go flex before you pay your industry dues, it may be harder to zip to the top of your chosen profession. And if you want more responsibility than collating quarterly reports, you have to put in as much face time at the office as (if not more than) everyone else—at least for a few years. Otherwise, you risk being treated like the gal "who doesn't value her career enough to show her face around here from 8 AM to 6 PM like the rest of us." And it could come back to haunt you at promotion time or during layoffs.

If you're a temp, congratulations! You're *always* first in line for layoffs and the last to know when the company makes critical policy changes that directly affect your job (even if said changes involve canning your supervisor). Still, if steering clear of long-term work relationships is a priority for you, being low woman on the corporate totem pole is a small price to pay.

DO YOU HAVE AN IMAGE PROBLEM?

It's the universal dilemma of side-giggers everywhere: Should you tell your boss and cubemates what you're up to after hours? If you have to ask, I'd say no. Better to err on the cautious side than have the entire office know you run a dick cozy–crocheting outfit in your basement. At my last (ultra-corporate) temp gig, I only told a select

Eight simple rules for negotiating flex work

Just because you'd like to set your own hours or work from home doesn't mean your employer will share the sentiment. Employers don't want to hear that you need a career makeover (or makeunder); they just want to know what's in it for them. To talk to the higher-ups at work about going flex, check out these recommendations from Cynthia Shapiro, author of *Corporate Confidential: 50 Secrets Your Company Doesn't Want You to Know—And What to Do About Them*.

1 . *Pay your dues.* Asking for a flex-work schedule after six to twelve months with a company is pushing it. You first have to prove yourself dependable, hardworking, and indispensable. Better to request flex work once you have three solid years under your belt—and have proven you can do your job backwards, forwards, blindfolded, and straitjacketed.

2 . *Win over your boss.* Make her look successful every step of the way, as if you're in business for yourself and she's your biggest client. Without her on your side, your bid for flex work won't get far. If you do score a flex arrangement, it's crucial that your boss support it 100 percent. Otherwise, you could drop your weekly hours from forty to twenty-four but still find yourself saddled with a full-time workload—only for less pay.

3 . *Be a company cheerleader.* Drink the Kool-Aid (or at least pretend to): If you plan to ask for the moon, resist the urge to publicly bad-mouth your employer. Sing the company's praises instead, especially in the office, where Big Brother really *is* watching.

4 . *Study the culture.* To predict how your employer will react to your request for flex, don't just study the policies in your employee manual—pay attention to the company's actions, too. "Look at what they truly reward and truly punish," Shapiro says. Is anyone else in your department working flexible hours, part-time, or from home?

Have any of your coworkers successfully negotiated flex work? Or was their request denied, or, worse, were they mysteriously let go?

5. *Don't go to HR.* When trying to figure out how your company will respond to your request for flex work, don't ask human resources for their opinion. "It's not safe," Shapiro says. If you do anything to make your company nervous, you're out the door; companies are too worried about lawsuits and the bottom line these days. Instead, talk to coworkers with flex-work options to see how they did it. Or get the advice of an industry organization like WashTech or Media Alliance, or your neighbor the HR rep (at another company, of course).

6. *Make your case in writing.* In your proposal, ask not what your company can do for you, but what you can do for your company: Offer to work flexibly for a trial period—perhaps telecommuting one or two days a week to start (but not Mondays, which are often busiest). Point out how your flex job will let you get more work done in less time, save the company cash, and any other (actual) benefits you can think of.

7. *Choose your timing wisely.* The best time to ask for a job makeover is when everything's calm, especially if you've just saved the day or somehow made your boss look fabulous. You don't want to request to go flex during a time of total chaos, like during a big product launch or when the company's fighting for its life—unless there's something irresistible in it for the company.

8. *Go the extra mile.* If you do go the part-time, flextime, or telecommuting route, regularly update your colleagues on your progress and stay on top of deadlines. (Even better, over-deliver the goods.) Keep in close contact with the mother ship at all times when working off-site. It's your job to assure your manager that everything's running swimmingly and you're not off in the Cayman Islands, sipping Mai Tais instead of working on the Big Presentation.

few about the articles I wrote on the side, since many of them had to do with working outside the cube.

Mistress Blue can relate. While it's a credibility booster to tell the bondage site she writes for that she's a working dominatrix, if she decides to write for a G-rated publication at some point, she'll likely stay mum about her alter ego. Same goes for Amy Lynwander, thirty-five, of Baltimore, who works for an engineering firm and runs a ghost-tour business on the side. "We're not supposed to have outside jobs," she says. "Plus, engineers and ghosts just don't seem to mix." Despite her best efforts to keep her side business under wraps, most of her coworkers know about it, probably because the local papers give the business a write-up every Halloween. On the flip side, Amy's business partner, Melissa Rowell, thirty-seven, talks openly about their ghost-chasing empire at her day job as a web designer. Not only does Melissa's boss support her side venture, he thinks it's a scream.

Sometimes up-and-coming entrepreneurs have to keep quiet about the bread-and-butter jobs they do to earn extra cash, too. If you're trying to make a go as a self-employed financial advisor or CPA, you won't want potential clients to see you pumping gas or ringing a register. A real estate agent I know from San Francisco had this dilemma before closing her first sale (agents work solely on commission). To pay her bills those first few months as an agent, she held down an evening restaurant gig. Besides worrying clients would bump into her at the restaurant, she worried they would not take her seriously if she told them she had a night job. So she kept her mouth shut (and closed her first sale in three months).

But what if the worst happens and one of your freelance clients—maybe an editor you write for or a client whose party you catered last weekend—catches you making sandwiches or ringing up women's underwear at your part-time gig? Even if you're dying on the inside, play it cool. A snappy quip like, "Don't tell my boss, but I'm researching a new [story/recipe/clothing line]," can help defuse the situation.

SHOW ME THE HEALTH INSURANCE

In the nineties, a friend of mine in San Francisco (let's call her Sondra) was balancing a part-time gig as a bookstore clerk with her fledgling enterprise caring for people's houseplants when she had to have an emergency appendectomy. Like a third of today's twentysomethings, she didn't have a stitch of health insurance. Not surprisingly, the staggering pile of hospital bills—upwards of $6,000, unrelenting due dates and all—drove her right into the arms of the full-time 9-to-5 world she'd been trying so hard to flee.

Take heed, anti 9-to-5er, and cover thine ass accordingly. I know I sound like your mom, but Sondra was healthy as a horse (just like you probably are) and never thought she'd have to deal with such a big pile of hospital bills in her twenties. Yes, funding a halfway decent health plan may mean scrimping and saving for a few more months while holding down a 9-to-5 gig before taking the flex-work plunge (that is, if your new gig won't include health insurance). But isn't it worth it, considering how badly one weekend in the hospital can screw up your plans to work outside the cube?

If you're cozying up to a temp agency, ask about what, if any, insurance plan they offer. Often you'll have to work for the agency a few weeks or months (depending on their rules and regs) before you're eligible for the health plan. And you may only be able to enroll in the plan during some tiny, predetermined window of time once or twice a year, so make sure you ask for the entire scoop. Don't rely on the agency to look out for you. Some will and some won't.

If you're thinking about leaving a job with insurance for one without, look into the COBRA plan offered by your soon-to-be-former employer. This includes part-timers and temps who get health coverage through their company (or temp agency). Under federal law, you can purchase the same health plan for up to eighteen months after quitting. If this is too pricey, or you never liked your plan to begin with, look into the professional associations in your field. Many offer decent packages at affordable rates, from national organizations like MediaBistro.com to regional ones like New York's FreelancersUnion.org. And depending on what state you live in, you may find private companies offering reasonably priced insurance policies for individuals (this is what I do, unless I'm on a temping tear, in which case I gladly accept my agency's health plan). You can scope out your state's offerings at www.AHIRC.org.

At the very least, get yourself some catastrophic health coverage, a bare-bones policy that will help with hospital fees should what happened to Sondra happen to you. If you fall on the super-organized end of the spectrum, you also may want to look into disability insurance, which pays you a "salary" if you're laid up for an extended period of time and can't work. This can be a lifesaver for self-employed folks.

SHOW ME THE MONEY

Before you make the leap to flex work, you of course need to figure out which type of flex job—if any—you can afford. This should entail taking a long, hard look at your monthly expenses and making sure you'd still be able to cover them with a smaller paycheck. Maybe you can't swing the 40 percent salary shrink that comes with lopping two days off your work week. So you go for the thirty-two-hour work week instead. Or you keep your forty-hour-a-week gig and ask for a day or two of weekly telecommuting, or to start your workday an hour earlier or later so you avoid rush-hour traffic. Gaining a couple hours a week is better than nothing.

If you're thinking of switching to a no-benefits work situation, be sure to factor in health insurance and retirement savings when determining how much change you can afford. If you're funding your retirement account (an IRA), experts recommend you put in the maximum you can afford. See a financial advisor if you're not so savvy with cash (even if, like me, your money maven is your mom). Lynn, the high-tech worker and volunteer mountain ranger, had a financial-planner pal help her with her goal of spending less so she didn't have to reduce her monthly retirement savings.

I talked about downsizing your spending in the first part of the book. Hopefully you're well on your way to driving less and biking, bussing, or carpooling more. Same goes for nixing all late-payment fees and bounced checks from your life. Ditto for buying used books, CDs, and clothes (or better yet, not buying at all). Cutting out cab rides, premium cable channels, and visits to the dry cleaner (easy remedy: stop buying "dry clean only" clothes) can save you a bundle, too, as can jettisoning that gym membership you haven't used in six months. So can getting your hair cut at the local beauty school (yes, I really do this) and eating all the food in your fridge before it liquefies or grows spores.

But don't stop there. Take inventory of your worldly possessions. If anything's collecting dust, sell it on eBay. From your Hello Kitty collection to that snowboarding equipment you haven't used since the nineties, chances are you're sitting on a pile of unclaimed cash. "I sold all my punk rock singles on eBay, and I paid my rent for a couple months," says Judy, the dating advice columnist. Clothes are a big untapped resource, too: If something in your closet still bears the price tag after a year, it's time you traded it in for some green. If eBay isn't your bag, hold a garage sale or take your castoffs to a consignment shop.

And finally, if you can't afford to go out, stay home. In case no one's pointed this out, you're not a Hilton. So the next time someone invites you to a swanky restaurant with entrées that cost more than you make in a week, practice the fine art of declining. Or say you have plans but will stop by for dessert. Or offer to host a potluck or meet your friends for a burrito instead, something more in line with your budget. Believe me, I've been there. Hell, I'm *still* there. None of your friends will hold it against you, and if they do, you're probably overdue for some new friends anyway.

ANTI 9-TO-5 ACTION PLAN

Fantasizing about a more flexible work schedule? These steps can help turn your daydreams into reality.

STAGE 1: SIZE UP YOUR CURRENT GIG	
Start date	**Checklist**
	If you're working many more hours a week than you were hired to, talk to your boss about lightening your load.
	If not, figure out what kind of makeover your day gig needs: Flexible hours? Less time at the office? A more relaxed corporate culture?
	Do the math: How much flex can you afford? Consider potential cuts to your paycheck and your benefits.

STAGE 2: DO THE DETECTIVE WORK	
Start date	**Checklist**
	Scope out the flex situation at your company by talking to those who've asked and received—and those who've been denied.
	Decide whether you'll try to negotiate a new arrangement with your employer or look for a new place of employ.
	If it's a new gig you want, you know the drill: homework, homework, homework.

STAGE 3: FINESSE YOUR REP	
Start date	**Checklist**
	If you're not on your boss's good side, get there—even if it takes six months or more.
	If planning to leave your day gig, update your resume as needed and make copies of all work samples.
	If planning to get by on your fallback skill during any unforeseen lean times, make sure your resume, portfolio, tools, and chops for said fallback skill are current.

STAGE 4: MAKE YOUR MOVE	
Start date	**Checklist**
	If you'll be forgoing benefits, get yourself some health insurance, even if it's just a catastrophic plan.
	If you'll be taking a pay cut, get militant about sticking to a budget and not wasting money. Enlist the help of a pal in the financial know if needed.
	Put your proposal for a more flexible work schedule in writing, get feedback from an HR-savvy friend, and plead your case with your boss.
	If leaving your day gig in the dust, begin interviewing for part-time, flex, or temp gigs.

chapter 5

I want to

work from

HOME

(but am afraid I wouldn't
get anything done)

"Where the hell are my slippers?"

—Megan Mullally as Karen Walker on *Will & Grace*

Contrary to popular belief, those of us who work from home do not lounge on our collective ass, eating bonbons and watching *General Hospital* and *Oprah* all day long. As mistresses of our own schedules, we must routinely beat our day planners into submission and ward off distraction, lest we blow our deadlines and fail to bring home the bacon.

Single mother Amanda Kelly is a shining example. When Amanda returned to the paid workforce after a nine-year hiatus, there was no doubt in her mind that she wanted to work from home. A thirty-seven-year-old Boston native and mother of five, Amanda wanted a gig that would get her closer to that elusive work/life balance. "I couldn't imagine some job where I'd be out of the house all day, every day," she says. Besides adding a truckload of stress to her life, commuting to work would mean far less time with her kids (a five-year-old, a seven-year-old, and eleven-year-old triplets). And paying to put her litter in after-school childcare would be, as she says, "insane." For her, using a "quilt of baby sitters" while working at her home office is infinitely more affordable.

So in 2004, after splitting from her husband, Amanda returned to work as a marketing and communications professional, where she'd left off almost a decade earlier. Only this time, she wasn't looking to work for a company; she was pounding the pavement for freelance projects. "I just networked the heck out of all these mothers I knew from school," asking if anyone had any leads, she says. Within six weeks, Amanda landed her first freelance project writing marketing copy. And in six months, she had the full thirty-hour work week (and income) she wanted, working in the comforts of her home.

So what exactly does working at home look like? For Amanda, an early riser, the day begins at 5 AM. She works in two-hour chunks, first stopping at 7 AM to feed the kids, shuttle them to school, and hit the gym. Back at her desk by 10 AM, she works till noon, at which time she takes lunch and engages her secret weapon, a thirty-minute power nap. Refreshed, she'll work for another couple hours until it's time to pick up the kids from school. Family time commences at about 3 PM, but if work is particularly nuts, Amanda squeezes in a couple more hours on the computer after the kids hit the hay. Happily, Amanda gets a break on weekends, when her supportive ex takes the kids off her hands. She uses this blessed "me" time to put the house back together, catch up with friends, go to her kids' sports games, and chill the heck out.

Amanda's schedule may sound a bit like boot camp, but it's much more manageable for her than working outside the home. Of course, mompreneurs don't hold a monopoly on working from home; like yours truly, many childfree women work from home because it gives us more time for our pet projects, be they short films, long novels, comic books, or political movements. It also gives us more time for—foreign-concept alert—ourselves.

We're not just talking about a few renegades here. In 2006, the U.S. Chamber of Commerce reported that one in six Americans worked from home at least one day a week. What's more, 30 percent of those lucky ducks were self-employed.

Being a virtual employee who telecommutes to a full-time, part-time, or temporary gig or a freelancer who runs her own business doesn't necessarily mean waking with the roosters like Amanda does. But it does require being your own drill sergeant. After all, if you don't goad yourself along, who will? This chapter will show you how to give yourself the structure you need to work all by your lonesome. Yes, if you have an employer breathing down your neck (or next of

Do you have the autonomy gene?

To see if you're hardwired to work independently as either an employee or a freelancer, check any of these homepreneurial skills you possess:

- ❑ Knowing when your right brain is most alert and showing up to work during those hours.

- ❑ Drawing a line in the sand (or across the living room) with roommates or family vying for your attention during said work schedule.

- ❑ Juggling multiple projects, managers, deadlines.

- ❑ Staying on top of the back-office duties of running your own business— invoicing, filing, and expense reporting, especially if you're the boss and the assistant.

- ❑ Hanging up on family and friends calling to shoot the breeze while bored at their office jobs or stuck in traffic. Better yet, screening all calls.

- ❑ Forsaking personal email, instant and text messaging, and web surfing during work hours—basically, going on a Tech Elimination Diet.

- ❑ Fishing for your own projects, from shamelessly promoting yourself to naming your price.

- ❑ Making water-cooler banter with your cat.

   If you checked a few items on this list, congrats—but don't dive into the homepreneur deep end just yet. Not everyone's cut out to work in solitude, and there's no shame in that. (There's probably more shame in the lengthy monologues I direct at my dog on a daily basis.) To see whether you can stand conversing with only your mail carrier each day, slowly ease into your home-based career. This chapter will tell you how.

   Note: If you get hives just reading this list, you may want to ditch the work-from-home idea. If it's a more flexible schedule you're after, check out the other flex options in Chapter 4. If it's self-employment you yearn for, perhaps working in a café or a (cheaply) rented office space would suit you better.

kin waiting for you to finish a conference call), you'll probably have an easier time staying on task than your freelance or childfree counterparts. But you'll still find tips here on working smarter and better balancing your work with your life. So, ready to march, soldier?

FOOLS RUSH IN

Women have been honing their cottage-industry skills for centuries, from preindustrial-era textile makers to New York housewives churning out grommets during World War II to today's kitchen-table activists, artists, administrators, financial planners, software developers, and web retailers (to name a few).

But that doesn't mean working from home is easy. With no bosses lurking about, there's less incentive to actually *do* your work. And with the couch in plain view (or perhaps even under your ass), motivation is a constant struggle. Work bleeds into life, life bleeds into work. Compartmentalization and organization are key. Isolation can be an enemy. On the flip side, you get the cushiest break room in town. You can do laundry while you work, curl up with your cat during breaks, even time lunch to coincide with fifteen minutes of *The Tyra Banks Show, Judge Judy,* or your crap-TV show of choice (as long as you can tear yourself away quickly).

Some people find working from home akin to water torture. Others who get a taste of the autonomous life have been known to shake their fist at the sky and dramatically proclaim, "As god is my witness, I'll never wear pantyhose again!"

"I love setting my own schedule," says Michelle Madhok, the founder of the personal-shopper site SheFinds.com. "I've had investors come along who want to give me money, but I'm grappling with that because I don't want someone telling me what to do."

Because working from home—not to mention for yourself—is new territory, do yourself a favor and resist the urge to rush in headlong. If you're negotiating a telecommuting deal with your boss, give it a whirl one or two days a week first. If you have your eye on self-employment, hold on to that day job and start freelancing on the side. If you need to wring more time from your schedule, see if you can negotiate a more flexible arrangement with your boss.

That's what Carolyn Anderson did. The thirty-three-year-old from Montreal was thoroughly burned out by her decade-long engineering career. So after taking a rash of sports medicine and fitness training classes, she reduced her day-gig hours to thirty a week and began working as a personal trainer on the side. The beauty of Carolyn's wading in slowly is that if she discovers she loathes (or sucks miserably at) being a solo artist, she has an income to fall back on. "It's a good, low-risk way for me to see if the business will work and build a client base," she says.

In the interest of wading in, don't rush to pimp your home office with all the latest gadgets and gizmos. Keep your spending to a minimum, and rent or borrow as much as you can. Why max out your credit card on a $750 executive desk when a garage-sale special will do the trick (or the company employing you will foot the bill)? If you're working for yourself, hold off on bells and whistles like a business checking account, bookkeeping software, and four-color promotional brochures your first few months. "It's almost like there's no point in setting that stuff up right away because you really don't know if it's going to work out," says Alona Esposito, twenty-eight, from Oakland, who owns and operates Diva Deals, a top-selling eBay store.

In Chapter 6 and the "Boss in a Box" section of the appendix, we'll talk about many of the meatier aspects of self-employment, from finding clients and negotiating rates to securing business licenses and paying your taxes. For now, though, let's focus on getting your home-based venture running like a well-oiled machine. Otherwise, all the business licenses, permits, and insurance in the world won't help you.

HOME IS WHERE THE DISTRACTION IS

People are always telling me, "I could never do what you do. I wouldn't have the discipline." They're right to suspect playing Deadline Dominatrix is key to working home alone, whether you report to an employer or run the show yourself. But they're wrong to think an old sloth can't learn new tricks. Case in point: me. As mistress of my own schedule for the past decade-plus, I know how easy it is to get sidetracked when trying do creative work in close proximity to all your books, magazines, computer games, junk mail, and DVDs, not to mention your bed, unmowed lawn, and the closet that won't stop screaming, "Organize me, damnit!"

My first year as a newbie freelancer, I spent half the day sleeping, the other half doing god knows what, and many an evening canceling social plans so I could cram to make the next morning's deadline. Fortunately, the concept of working smarter finally sunk in after what I now like to think of as The Self-Yelp Incident. I'd put off proofreading an 800-page self-help book—a plum assignment from a rosy new client with deep pockets—until the last possible weekend before the due date (never mind the ten-pound tome had been collecting dust on my desk for a month). Rather than blow my deadline (at least I had *some* sense back then), I plowed through personal-growth gobbledygook for forty hours straight (as in, no sleep for two days) in order to finish the job by Monday morning. Talk about masochism. Not to mention irony.

Although I wasn't instantly cured of my pesky problem of putting off for tomorrow what I could chip away at today, I got on the road to recovery and began cracking my own whip. Honestly, it doesn't take long to realize the more soap-opera marathons and three-hour lunches with unemployed friends you indulge in, the less rent money you have. These days, if I'm burning the midnight oil, it's almost always because a job too good to pass up came along and I was willing to work the extra hours to squeeze it in. The point is, the sooner you put your projects to bed, the sooner you can get on with your day or evening—which is probably the main reason you wanted to telecommute or work for yourself in the first place. It may sound obvious, yet so many freelancers—rookies and old salts alike—will tell you they grapple with the same deadline demons, even when it means they're putting off getting paid and jeopardizing their projects or, worse, their reputation. In fact, many of my *clients* have told me it can be tough to find freelancers who do a decent job and meet their deadlines.

In Chapter 3, we talked about how to wrangle your after-hours schedule so you can get down to the business of getting your creative work done. Writing a few pages of your novel in the morning before dashing off to your office job is one thing. But prodding yourself along as an at-home worker for six or eight hours a day is an entirely different beast. "It's hard to push yourself and realize that no one's going to provide the structure for you," says Michelle, the SheFinds.com founder. "Sometimes I just want to sit on the couch. I mean, the couch is pretty close by." Of course, once you realize that if you nap on the couch, you don't eat, motivation comes pretty quickly.

If you have kids, you're probably more adept than the rest of us at getting down to business, thanks to such non-negotiable hard stops as "twenty minutes till they wake up from their nap" and "two hours till I have to pick them up from daycare." If you're a mom, you may even be wondering why I'm going on and on about this time-management stuff. Still, if the kids are at school for the next six hours, or your househusband (or housewife) has your infant covered for the next eight, that's a pretty big window you, too, could potentially piss away.

So whether you live with kids, adults, dogs, cats, canaries, or just the dust bunnies under the bed, the next section will give you ideas for staying on top of your paid work (sorry, I'm no help with household chores). You'll also get ideas for keeping your roommates—especially the waist-high ones—out of your hair when you're on deadline, and for being an all-around beacon of efficiency. Maintaining your telecommuting arrangement or freelance clients depends on it.

According to a recent Salary.com survey, 45 percent of cube-dwellers cite surfing the web as their preferred procrastination tactic. Sound like anyone you know? If so, it's time to cut the digital cord (cell, email, and IM addicts, this means you, too). Unplugging frees up a sizable chunk of your at-home workday, unless, of course, being available at a moment's notice is part of your job. As a recovering email-holic, I fully admit to taking a hit off my inbox first thing in the morning, before lunch, and at the end of the day. I have a "look but don't touch" policy during the workday, though: No replies allowed (not even one word), and absolutely no clicking of links. The second I start writing people back or surfing the web, it's all over— I'm doomed to distraction for an hour or two, time I could have spent chipping away at my actual *paying* work.

THE SEVEN HABITS OF HIGHLY EFFECTIVE HOMEPRENEURS

The reason I'm paying a lot of lip service to becoming the productivity poster child is that your home is, first and foremost, the place where you kick back and try to forget everything you had to do that day to make rent and grocery money. Your apartment or house wasn't necessarily built to accommodate a one-woman cottage industry. It was built for relaxing, goofing off, loving, bathing, slacking, and sleeping.

If you want to succeed at this work-at-home thing, you have to spend some time premeditating where and when you'll don your "on duty" hat, how you'll set up shop, and how you'll stay connected with the outside professional world. This may sound like elementary stuff, but newbie telecommuters and freelancers ask me questions like this all the time. If you, too, are curious about what a day in the life of a successful at-home worker looks like, read on.

Habit 1: Get routine.

If you're a telecommuting employee, your company will likely dictate what hours you have to work. But if you're self-employed, setting "office hours" will help you stay on top of your workload and better compartmentalize when you're off duty—something that's infinitely harder to do when your office is ten feet down the hall.

Without set hours, it's far too easy to fall prey to the "I'll just take the afternoon off and then work late into the evening or get up before dawn to finish" line of thinking. Half the time you're too tired to do the work justice after dinner, let alone drag your sorry, procrastinating ass to your desk. And setting your clock for 4 AM to finish the work you blew off yesterday is a surefire recipe for over-sleeping. Instead, I like to work from nine till six, with lunch and an hour-long walk with my pooch somewhere in between. As far as I'm concerned, playing hooky is the exception, not the rule.

Setting firm hours signals to your office-bound clients and col-leagues that you're a pro. It also prevents workaholic clients from calling you at 10 PM or instant-messaging you at 6 AM, both of which have happened to me. As long as your clients don't work 24/7, try your best to mirror their hours. They'll want to know you're available when they need you, not three days later. If you live in Walla Walla, Washington, but mainly work with Wall Street firms, this may mean starting your day a tad earlier. The more seriously you take your job, the more your customers will, too.

Because you now have the shortest commute imaginable, it can be tempting to work every waking minute. But nothing screams "My job is my whole life!" more than rolling out of bed and checking your email before you even brush your teeth. Just as you did when you had an office gig, you need a morning ritual before "heading off to work," whether it's getting jacked up on espresso at the corner café or rocking out to the *Nine to Five* movie soundtrack. Some freelancers can't get down to business without a shower and fresh underwear. Others can't work without slipping into something more office-y, from the button-up blouse and pleated pants right down to the belt, shoes, and lipstick. Your morning ritual helps you keep work in that nice, neat little box where it belongs—far, far away from your leisure time.

If you live with kids, working the same hours each week will make dealing with daycare a hell of a lot easier—whether your partner watches the kids, a baby sitter comes over, or you drop them off at a kiddie-care center. Letting the family know Mom works every day from 9 AM till 3 PM can also help keep any roomies at bay, except maybe those four-legged ones.

Habit 2: Mark your territory.

In Chapter 3, we talked about claiming a workspace of your own when trying to get a side project off the ground. When you work at home as your *main* gig, this is even more crucial. It bears repeating: One of your biggest jobs as a homepreneur is to avoid any and all distractions like the plague, from the other people milling about your home to the stinky dishes in the sink, the dog whining for a walk, the incessant telemarketers, even the Jehovah's witnesses ringing your bell.

One of the best ways to stay focused is to stake your claim on a room with a door that shuts, even if, as author Kristin Rowe-Finkbeiner says, "it's the size of a closet." Hell, Steven King worked in his laundry room for years. The beauty of the shuttable door is that it (a) helps keep out unwanted noise and visitors, (b) ensures no one messes with any projects you're in the middle of when you're away from your desk, and (c) makes workaholism less tempting.

Closing the office door gives you some separation of church and state, much needed for those who work at home. If, however, that shuttable door isn't doing much to deter you from the mound of dishes in your sink during work hours, you may want to revisit those procrastination-busters on page 62.

Habit 3: Pimp your virtual office.

Once you start working at home in earnest, take the time to trick out your workspace before those deadlines hit, from your desk and electronic equipment to your filing cabinet and supply stash. This doesn't mean buying spendy equipment you'll only use once a year (and could otherwise find at FedEx Kinko's), like a $5,000 industrial-strength color copier. It does mean getting yourself the furniture you need to work comfortably and the tools you'll use on a weekly basis. Trust me, customers and coworkers do not want to hear you missed a deadline because your Stone Age computer's on the fritz or your dial-up service is hinky. Outfit yourself with the proper gear, and your colleagues will find you as professional as your khaki'd, commuting counterparts (even if you do work in Catwoman pajamas).

Don't stop at the new(ish), reliable computer system and high-speed Internet connection, though. Get yourself a land line or an ultra-reliable cell phone for work calls and work calls alone. If you see a fair amount of faxing in your future, set up a dedicated phone line for that too, or get some fax software. If you live with anyone shorter than your waist, a phone with a mute button can be a lifesaver. Ditto for caller ID, which helps you screen out telemarketers and retired relatives; voice mail, which helps you haul ass on deadline without distraction; and call forwarding to your cell, which allows you to leave the batcave without missing a caller you've been expecting.

If you're self-employed, rent a PO Box so your checks don't get ripped off and you don't have to put your home address on your business cards or website. Also, scope out a quiet café with decent parking where you can meet with clients passing through town or those who don't have a physical office of their own. It's far more professional than meeting in your kitchen.

Habit 4: Stay on top of administrata.

If I can't find the research I printed out last week for an article I'm writing on a tight deadline, I wind up wasting precious time hunting for it in the two-foot mound of papers on my desk. For that reason, I try not to let my filing (or invoicing, bookkeeping, or business correspondence) pile up too long.

ANTI 9 to 5 tip

It doesn't matter if you're a telecommuting employee or a freelancer—take the time to create an ongoing filing system for your expense receipts. You'll need to know where you hid the suckers when your company expense reports or annual tax returns come due. I stash all my gas, research, office supply, and business lunch receipts in one of those nerdy accordion files and tally them by category in a pretty spreadsheet. Before I started doing this, I usually lost most of my receipts, which meant I lost money. Stay current with your boss about which expenses your company reimburses or, if you're self-employed, with your tax preparer or IRS.gov about which are tax deductible.

On an ideal, procrastination-free day, I'll wait till 4 or 5 PM, when I'm done writing or editing, to return any work-related phone or email messages that have piled up. I save my weekly filing and invoicing, probably the most mindless tasks in my repertoire, for Sunday nights camped out in front of the tube. If I have a rash of email replies to write, I'll tackle them in one weekly sitting, usually on a Monday or Wednesday evening.

Clustering similar admin chores together—even making a weekly or monthly calendar appointment with yourself to tackle them—can help keep the thicket down. Besides, life is so much sweeter when you get your creative work done during the hours when your synapses are actually firing and save the admin work for those times when you're less fresh. Whether you're a night owl or a morning glory, the idea is to give yourself a concentrated chunk of uninterrupted time for your heavy "thinking" work (be it drafting blueprints, building an online store, or writing a grant proposal).

Habit 5: Press the flesh.

One of the biggest pitfalls of working at home is the isolation. "Working at home by yourself makes you a little crazy," says New York–based freelance writer Judy McGuire. I'm certainly no exception to the madness. Woe is the person who catches me on the phone or my doorstep at the end of the day. It doesn't matter if it's my sister, my boyfriend, or the UPS delivery gal—I'll regale my unwitting audience with scintillating tales of how many typos I caught or times I cracked open the thesaurus that day.

The good news is, there's an easy remedy for the loneliness and cabin fever that come with being the Macaulay Culkin of the work world: Crawl out of your cave every so often. And I don't just mean to answer the phone or your email. If you have an employer, convene with your coworkers once a week, once a month, or once a quarter, even if it's not part of your job description. Same goes for self-employed types with local clients. Showing your face every so often is just good business. Besides, it gives you a reason to bathe.

Joining a professional organization is another way to combat the monotony of working alone at home. Number one, it looks good on your resume. Number two, going to monthly industry events gives you a chance to talk shop with someone other than your cat, not to mention a compelling reason to change your underwear. Number three, if you're self-employed, it's one of the best ways to get business tips and job leads. As you saw in Part I of the book, organizations supporting career women and business owners of all vocations abound; find one or two you like and get to know the locals.

Scheduling coffee dates with friends and other women who work at home can help with that much-needed camaraderie and structure, too. But be careful you don't go overboard. It's much too easy for a power lunch with a fellow freelancer to turn into a three-hour event, once you factor in the travel time, the fact that someone always arrives late because of a "work emergency," and the obligatory post-meal "I don't want to go back to work yet" latte. When all is said and done, your afternoon is pretty much shot. And if those are your most productive hours, well, you do the math. So unless you live down the street from each other and can make it snappy, I'd keep social lunches to a minimum or skip them altogether. Better to get all your work done first and meet up at the end of the day for happy hour or dinner.

Habit 6: Work the web.

If you work for yourself, a website—even if it's just one page—is a must. For starters, working the web will make you feel more professional. Besides, potential customers like to see that a freelancer has an online home. It says that Good with Numbers, Computer Doctor, or Human Resources Diva isn't some title you dreamed up for yourself yesterday. Use your site to tell would-be customers a bit about the services you offer, your qualifications, and your other clients.

Some freelancers offer a full resume on their site; others stick with a prose-format bio and client list. If you provide a creative service like web illustration or newsletter writing, be sure to post or link to your best samples. If you're not sure how to set up your site, cruise the webpages of other freelancers in your line of work.

To customers, your website is the business equivalent of proof that their online date doesn't have three heads. Case in point: Christa Fleming, thirty-six, a freelance graphic designer who works from her Seattle-area home, gets loads of calls from potential clients who were referred to her but stopped to look her up online first. They'll tell her, "I was just looking at your website . . ." and then proceed to rattle off which of her design samples they liked most.

A slick website won't get you far, though, if no one knows about it. To get the word out, list your site with as many big search engines as you can (you know, Google, Yahoo!). If you have no idea how to do this, sites like AddMe.com and SearchEngineWatch.com can help school you. Or ask a couple web-savvy pals (but save the instructions so you'll know what to do next time). Trade links with like-minded freelancers, too. And if any professional organizations you've joined offer free listings in their online directory, take them up on this. Businesses in need of freelancers use the web like a virtual phone book all the time, so it's in your best interest to list yourself in as many places as possible.

Like I said earlier in the book, avoid posting anything to your site, blog, or photo gallery (or anywhere else on the web) you wouldn't want clients to see. I know a freelance erotica writer who's got some lovely nudes of herself on her site. In her line of work, this hardly raises an eyebrow—in fact, it's probably great PR. But if you're a CPA or HR pro, baring your derriere online isn't going to earn you any Brownie points (or business). My rule of thumb: If it's not something I'd want my mother to see, it's not something I want my customers to see.

Habit 7: Keep your resume and portfolio current.

Before I had a website and got wise to updating my resume regularly, it never failed: I'd be busy beyond belief when some hotshot company would ask to see my resume and writing samples. So, despite my already-stretched-to-the-max schedule, I'd scramble to add six months' worth of projects to my resume and convert the corresponding writing samples to digital files. Obviously, taking time once a month or so to spruce up your promo materials can save you from such last-minute crunches. Sure, I could have sent along my resume as is, along with some older writing samples, but my most recent projects are usually the ones I want to show off.

If you're not sure how to structure a freelance resume, again, poke around the websites of solo workers you admire. A few suggestions from my arsenal of resume-writing tactics: Don't use an "objective" on a freelance resume (as in, "To be the best damn freelance proofreader this side of Texas"); it will just sound amateurish, like you're not yet doing what your resume professes you do for a living. Do include a summary sentence or paragraph at the top that explains you're a freelancer who specializes in whatever you specialize in and has whatever unique skills you have.

If you've done too many freelance projects to list on one page, take a bow—and then select the biggest and best clients to include on your resume. Unless you're the secretary of state or a tenured professor, no one wants to wade through thirteen pages of your achievements. Better to keep your resume to one or two pages and indicate that highlights from your illustrious freelance career follow, and that you'd be happy to provide a full client list and references upon request (make sure you actually have these items at your fingertips). And do include any relevant 9-to-5 gigs on your freelance resume; people will want to see what you did in your previous life.

MOTHER'S LITTLE HELPER

Naps, school, childcare, or a househusband (or housewife) will only get you so far. If you're a mom who works from home, like my tech-editor pal Kelly, you're probably more than familiar with life-and-death distractions of the "Can we go to Australia before I'm thirteen?" or "Listen to this really funny line from *Cheaper by the Dozen 2*" nature.

So how do you keep the little ones out of your hair while working, besides popping in a Pixar flick? Since my only child has a tail and four legs, I asked work-at-home moms raising everything from human preschoolers to teens for their secrets. Their top suggestion: Give your kids some quality time before sitting down at your desk. "If I focus on reading a story one on one or playing a game first, my kids are much more likely to play independently for a while without needing me," says Julie van Amerongen, thirty-nine, a freelance publicist in Eugene, Oregon, with two preschoolers and a musician husband who's frequently on tour.

A little conditioning goes a long way, too. Amanda, the single mother of five you met at the start of the chapter, says her children do a brilliant job of not disturbing her when the office door is shut, her signal that Mom's on the phone. And Julie seconds the law-of-the-land approach: "My kids understand that when I'm sitting at my desk they have to say, 'Excuse me,' and that they're more on their own."

Finally, stashing some prized toys in your office can work wonders. "Anything interactive that doesn't require too much on your end" does the trick, Julie says, whether it's a peewee worktable and art supplies or Legos and train tracks. One freelancer I know keeps an Xbox in her office. But you needn't have a fat budget to keep the kids occupied. "There was a period of time when a mountain of pennies and a piggy bank would buy me a good, uninterrupted fifteen minutes," Julie says. And Kristin Rowe-Finkbeiner, coauthor of *The Motherhood Manifesto*, says, "My business cards are probably used more for making houses for action figures than for networking."

How to smell a scam

In 1965, two dozen New York housewives were arrested for taking phone messages in their homes for a team of bookies. None of these hapless gals had any previous criminal history. They'd simply responded to a newspaper ad promising they'd make $50 to $100 a week for jotting down some names and phone numbers (they never took any actual bets). In fact, many of the women thought they were working for traveling salesmen.

While today's work-at-home scams look a bit different, the premise hasn't changed much over the years: You work from home for far fewer hours than everyone else you know (the poor suckers!), and by barely lifting a finger, you make a mint, earning you fast cars, big boats, and tropical time-shares. But there's no such thing as a get-rich-quick gig. Those medical billing, craft assembly, and envelope stuffing gigs you always see advertised? Totally bogus, says the Federal Trade Commission. Those make-a-killing-off-the-Internet ads? More of the same.

Not convinced? Then chew on this: Alona Esposito, the eBay power-seller and MBA you met earlier, works forty hours a week on Diva Deals, her eBay store. Although her business pulls in $20,000 a month, after paying out all expenses (including taxes), she walks away with a monthly salary of $2,000—and works a part-time job on weekends to make extra cash. It took her three years to turn a significant, consistent profit, a pretty standard business statistic.

So how can you tell if your supposed dream gig is a dud? If you heard about it from a TV infomercial or in an online ad claiming you can "Earn $$$$$ from home!" Or if the ad lacks any company name, website, or physical address. Or if it arrived in your inbox. Or you call the number mentioned in said ad and get a lengthy recording riddled with sports clichés and phrases like "wealth-generating program," "Earn thousands per day," and "I got rich and you can, too." Or you're told you have to attend a workshop, buy a product, send money, or fork over your bank account information before you even know what the gig entails.

Before you get into bed with a client or employer you've never heard of, check them out with the Better Business Bureau (www.bbb.org). If you're not sure something's a scam, consult the Federal Trade Commission (www.ftc.gov) or ScamBusters.org. If a gig sounds too good to be true, it probably is.

SHOW ME THE MONEY

If you telecommute to a staff gig, have your employer pay for as much of your home office equipment as possible. Stay on top of filing your expense receipts and reports so you collect any reimbursements you're due. If you work from home as a freelancer, you can ask clients to pay for reasonable project expenses (more about charging clients in the next chapter). A copywriter may charge for international research or conference calls. A publicist may charge for postage. An accountant may want reimbursement for overnight shipping costs. Of course, you can't expect your clients to pay for your paper clips, printer cartridge, or ergonomic chair. As a freelancer, the overhead's on you.

Business advisors will tell you to save at least a year's worth of living expenses before you go solo. But most mere mortals don't make enough money to sock away even a couple months' rent. That's why growing your home-based business on the side while you keep a part-time, flex, or even full-time job is your best bet. Maxing out your credit cards is your worst. Take it from someone who's learned the hard way: If you rely on your credit cards to fill in the financial gaps and things don't go according to plan, not only will you be out of work, but you might owe the bank more money than your last annual salary.

A big part of wading in slowly is keeping your start-up costs down. Buy only those tools and supplies you need on a weekly basis: computer, desk, hammer, nails, chain saw, whatever. Borrow or rent the rest. Wherever possible, look to discount and secondhand stores, wholesalers, bulk retailers, holiday sales, craigslist, Freecycle.org, bartering, and haggling to help you cut costs. If one of your friendly local businesses is closing its doors, wish them luck—then see if they're selling off any furniture or office equipment. Ask your friends with corporate jobs to scour their company classifieds or bulletin boards for deals for you, too. If you need help with your resume or website, you know the drill: barter, barter, barter.

A couple caveats about bargain shopping: If you're buying a computer, it's worth the investment to get one with a warranty, good customer support, and a local repair center. These days, you can get a brand-spanking-new computer for a few hundred clams. Joy! Also, take it from someone who single-handedly kept her chiropractor in business last year: Don't skimp on the comfortable chair. Take solace in knowing that any office equipment or work gear you need to run your business can be a tax deduction (although unless you're an actress, new clothes and dry cleaning don't count).

I know this can be a lot of detail to digest, so deep breaths, okay? We'll talk much more about it all in the next chapter.

ANTI 9-TO-5 ACTION PLAN

Want to join the ranks of women who work from home in fuzzy slippers? Whether you telecommute to a salaried gig or run your own business, here's what you need to do to set yourself up properly. Like I said, we'll delve more deeply into playing boss and taking your solo venture to the next level in the next chapter.

STAGE 1: TRICK OUT YOUR HOME OFFICE	
Start date	Checklist
	Designate a private, distraction-proof space with a shuttable door as your office.
	Get the office equipment and supplies you need (on sale, of course), including a dedicated phone line and comfy chair.
	Make sure your computer is in tip-top shape and operates at warp speed.
	If self-employed, rent a PO Box and scope out a public place to meet clients.

STAGE 2: BEAT YOUR SCHEDULE INTO SUBMISSION	
Start date	Checklist
	Come up with realistic office hours you can stick to and your employer or clients will support.
	Clue in coworkers, customers, and/or roommates to your set hours.
	If prone to digital distractions, practice turning off the phone and modem for an hour a day (and working up to a half and then a whole day).

STAGE 3: GET ANAL	
Start date	Checklist
	Set up a filing system for all paperwork and expenses.
	Pick the days and hours of the week you'll devote to filing, invoicing, correspondence, and other administrata. Start this week.

STAGE 4: GET YOUR PROMO ON	
Start date	Checklist
	Make inexpensive business cards and letterhead.
	Update your resume and portfolio. Rinse and repeat every three months (easier to remember if you note in your calendar).
	Build your website and list it with search engines.
	Schedule some weekly face time with coworkers, clients, and industry colleagues.

chapter 6

I want to be
my own
BOSS

"So long, you wage slaves!"

—Rosalind Russell as Hildegaard Johnson in *His Girl Friday*, 1940

My decision to become my own boss at age twenty-four stemmed from a number of resentments. My seemingly lobotomized manager. The empty promises of a raise. The mice that ran rampant in the Manhattan office where I worked. The scowling passengers crammed into subways like thighs in support hose. Oh, and the fact I considered 9 AM the middle of the night. Most people would suck it up and stick out the 9-to-5 life a few years, maybe a decade—at least until they're sure they have enough experience or clout to strike out on their own. I, on the other hand, had a bit of a rebel complex, which meant I had a nasty habit of leaping first and looking later.

I wish could credit my brilliant business plan as the reason I didn't go belly up within the first six months as a freelance writer. Truth is, I didn't know the first thing about running my own business, as evidenced by the fact that I quit my job with no clients, portfolio, or savings to speak of. To compensate for this, I became the queen of yes, agreeing to all projects that came my way. In fact, I pretty much eliminated "no" from my vocabulary. And that landed me a lot of work. When asked if I minded writing about colonics, adult acne, or erectile dysfunction, I gave new meaning to the phrase "unbridled enthusiasm." If a client needed me to work fourteen-hour days, weekends, even New Year's Eve, I was their gal. If told, "We'd love to hire you, but we can only afford half the [bargain basement] price you quoted us. . . ." I'd roll over without thinking twice. If they asked for seventeen sets of rewrites, I'd smile sweetly and say, "No problem." Never mind all the extra work would reduce my wage to just pennies an hour.

Despite my best efforts—or perhaps because of them—my freelance income didn't clear the poverty level for several years. But I had tasted sweet freedom and had no intention of looking back. Short of earning a rap sheet, I did whatever it took to fund my freelance habit. To fill the pay gaps, I scavenged for part-time temp and nanny gigs. I ate Top Ramen and tuna for breakfast, lunch, and dinner. I knew what time of day all the supermarkets within a five-mile radius put out their free samples. Looking back, this was clearly not the way to go.

When my profits finally began to perk up, I became more discriminating, turning down the crappier gigs and raising my rates. I also caught on to a few valuable business concepts: contracts that clearly outlined what I would and wouldn't do—and how much it would cost. Minimum fees, rush fees, and late-payment fees. Getting paid a portion of my fee up front. Checking my client's references to make sure they were good for the money. Building a specialty. Promoting myself shamelessly. Seeking the advice of those who knew a hell of a lot more than I did about self-employment taxes, copyright law, and financial planning. Having a fallback skill I could run to if the cash cow croaked (or came down with a case of mad downsizing disease).

I learned every last bit of it by trial and error, basically by bumping into walls. I couldn't agree more with Maggie Kleinpeter, co-owner of the online craft and clothing boutique Supermaggie, when she says, "You'll probably learn more from your mistakes than from doing it right."

While one chapter can't cover every detail of starting a small business, it will give you the lowdown on the questions people ask me most about working for myself. It doesn't matter if you're a web designer, sock-monkey maker, or the Maytag repairwoman; working solo is working solo. Consider this your crash course in getting there as simply and cheaply as humanly possible, whether you're just doing some preliminary research or gearing up to take your side gig to the next level.

THE FINE PRINT

I 'll give it to you straight: Even when you do everything right, working for yourself looks absolutely nothing like the six-days-off-a-week, forever-adding-to-your-$250,000-wardrobe life of Carrie Bradshaw on *Sex and the City*. Sure, you can work in your lingerie (or flannel PJs, the Seattle freelance uniform of choice). But Carrie's seemingly nonexistent workload and bottomless shoe budget? Total fabrication. I mean, that could be you several years (or decades) down the line. But don't expect it right out of the dressing room.

"Your first year, it's really, really hard to turn a profit," says Sharon Miller, CEO of the Renaissance Entrepreneurship Center in San Francisco, which offers small-business training to women and minorities and was one of the country's first microenterprise-development programs. Experts say that on average it can take up to three years before you start seeing a profit. Then again, if you're being paid to provide a freelance service out of your home, such as writing computer code or editing catalog copy, and you have minimal start-up and business expenses, you should see a profit within a matter of weeks or months.

For Searah Deysach, owner of Early to Bed, a women-positive sex shop in Chicago, that first year in business was one of the longest, hardest years of her life. But the thirty-two-year-old art-school dropout was hell-bent on making a go of a gig she believed in, so she toughed out those first humbling twelve months and tried to remember to count her blessings. "I was very happy to not have to smell like coffee every night, or to not have to worry about some asshole boss."

On your best days as a small-business owner, you'll feel like a girl in pigtails, making macaroni art in the basement after grammar school, grinning until your cheeks ache and squealing, "I can't believe I get paid to do this!" On your worst days, you'll feel like the biggest idiot in the world for not having paid sick days, vacation time, and free health insurance. Customers will cancel orders, stiff you, or go under. Computers will die mercilessly on the eve of a huge presentation or, if you run a retail business, during the holiday crunch. You'll work through the night or a bad flu to make big deadlines. You'll make stupid, costly mistakes. You'll do loads of administrative work you can't bill anyone for. You'll have dry spells that last for weeks. You'll worry about money incessantly, sometimes instead of sleeping at night. At times, you'll struggle to stay motivated, disciplined, awake. You'll feel lonely. And you'll wonder if you were insane to strike out on your own in the first place.

"I have that little breakdown at least once every two weeks," says Supermaggie's Maggie Kleinpeter. "I'll be up late finishing an order and think, *If I had a 9-to-5 job, I'd be asleep by now, but instead I'm up at 10:30 working.* Then I remind myself that if I had a 9-to-5 job, I'd have to go in to the office tomorrow."

Of course, you can't beat the perks: Every cent you make goes into your own empire (or pocket). You set your own hours. Name your price. Choose who you work with and what projects you take on. Crash through the glass ceiling. Get your work done in three-quarters the time it would take in some email-saturated, meeting-happy cube farm. Take your kids to the park, Fridays off, or ninety-minute midday yoga breaks. Work in the muumuu you slept in—for the past four days—because, as She-E-O of your own enterprise, you call the shots now.

TAKE A FLYING LEAP, BUT WEAR A HELMET

"I have been waiting for the last eight years for some kind of epiphany or some kind of sign to tell me what I should be doing with my life," says Carolyn Anderson, thirty-three, the Seattle engineer who recently cut back her day-job hours to start a fitness-training business on the side. "I finally realized that I'm 80 percent sure that I want to be a personal trainer, and if I was 100 percent sure, I'd already be one. It recently dawned on me that I'm never going to be 100 percent sure, so I should just try it."

ANTI 9 to 5 tip

Having a fallback skill can be a lifesaver, especially if it's a skill that can't be offshored, like repairing refrigerators or editing marketing copy. Offering customers a proven service or product that isn't necessarily your first choice can get you out of the cube faster—and help line your (handmade, appliquéd) change purse during those early, lean months. To make ends meet her first year in business, Erika Teschke, the dog-walker you met earlier in the book, took on extra overnight pet-sitting gigs, even though it meant lengthy stays away from her husband and four dogs. By her second year, her customer base was so big, she started turning away the overnight gigs.

Going solo is a combination of wearing as much protective gear as you can and then taking a running jump like Carolyn did, even if your knees are knocking. Yes, you want to arm yourself with as much know-how and cash as possible. But you don't want to drag out the planning phase until the next millennium. That's what's known as stalling. This obviously won't be an overnight process. It could take a few months; it could take a couple years. It just shouldn't take a lifetime.

Contrary to popular belief, you don't need to inherit a windfall from long-lost Aunt Hortence to start a business. There's such a thing as starting small. And starting small means you can start *sooner*. Launching your business on the side while keeping your 9-to-1 or 9-to-5 paycheck, like Carolyn's doing, frees you from worrying about how you'll cover pesky little items like groceries and running water. It also allows you to hone your chops on someone else's dime. "I learn tremendous amounts for my own business by working for a larger company," says clothing designer Brett Lally. Although the thirty-two-year-old New Yorker launched Borne, her own clothing collection, in 2005, she continued to hold down a three-day-a-week gig designing clothes for someone else to feed her bank account and boost her expertise.

Starting small also means there's less at stake: If, after a couple years, your business takes a nosedive or you realize you'd rather eat crow than play boss, you don't stand to lose (or repay) as much cash as if you'd taken out a hefty bank loan. Don't think of going solo as opening yourself up to potential failure—think of it as a big fat learning experience. Considering you'll likely be working twenty, thirty, or forty more years, rolling the dice on a solo career—especially before you're bound by a mortgage or little mouths to feed—doesn't seem like such a big gamble. If you lose your shirt, the cube farm and all its perks will still be there. "There's no reason not to try it," says Searah, the sex-toy purveyor. "I felt like I didn't know what I was doing, I had no money, and I also knew that if I didn't try it, even if I failed miserably and had to pay for it for the rest of my life, I would regret it."

MBA TO GO

You hear the statistic over and over: Seven out of ten businesses close their doors within the first five years. There's no guarantee you'll be among the lucky ones who make it, but the more prepared you are, the better chance you stand of staying out of the sardines aisle.

"In a lot of art fields, people get this degree in writing or fine art or something, and it's almost as if the school didn't want to approach the business part of it," says Linda Ross, thirty-five, a freelance costume and lighting designer for theaters around the country. "And

Fempreneurs on the rise

In 2006, the Economic Policy Institute reported that the average U.S. CEO earns 262 times the average worker, making more money in one workday than the typical peon makes all year. If you ask me, that's reason enough to strike out on your own. Although just 3 percent of women-owned businesses in America earn $1 million or more in annual revenues, women entrepreneurs are a force to be reckoned with. Behold these stats from the Center for Women's Business Research:

- One in eleven adult women in America is an entrepreneur.

- A total of 10.6 million women in the country—comprising almost half of all privately held businesses—hawk their art, products, and services. These companies employ 19.1 million people and rack up almost $2.5 trillion in sales.

- One in five privately held, women-owned companies is owned by women of color, and women of color own 36 percent of all firms owned by persons of color.

- Between 1997 and 2004, while women-owned firms expanded into all industries, they grew the most in the construction, transportation, communications, public utilities, and agricultural services industries.

then you get out in the real world and you realize you need accounting and bookkeeping and stuff like that."

The good news is, successful business ownership is not some exclusive country club populated only by Harvard MBAs. In fact, women-owned businesses are growing at almost twice the rate of all U.S. companies. To join these ranks, you need to channel your inner She-E-O and crank up your business savvy. This section will help you get started. (For some of the nittier, grittier details of self-employment, see the "Boss in a Box" section in the appendix.)

Know thy market

Opening that quaint little knick-knack boutique à la Juliette Binoche in *Chocolat* sounds sweet, especially if you throw in the fling with Johnny Depp. But it's not enough to be passionate about your business idea. You need to know if anyone will buy what you're selling and how much they're willing to pay for it. Without a viable service or commodity that inspires people to part with their hard-earned dollars, you don't have a business.

If you're already selling your goods on the side (and your customers are clamoring for more), you're ahead of the game. If not, or if you're looking to expand, you need to do the market research. Start by bestowing your crocheted toilet-paper cozies upon your family for Chrismukah or poop-scooping their back yard in exchange for a pile of change (or a hot meal). Note their reactions, as well as those of their neighbors. Show your portfolio to objective friends and colleagues and get their honest feedback. Set up a table at an event like the Renegade Craft Fair in Brooklyn or Chicago, your local farmers market, or a business trade show, and sell, baby, sell.

Talk to everyone you can; see what they like or loathe. Send out an informal email survey, asking your target market what they think of your service and how much they'd pay for it. Go business to business or door to door if you have to. The U.S. Census Bureau website (www.census.gov) and your local chamber of commerce (easy to find on www.uschamber.com) can also help fill in the blanks about your target customers—for example, by giving statistics on their disposable income and propensity to spend.

Do I really need a business plan?

Yes, you really do need a *written* business plan. Now, before you slam this book shut, hear me out: A business plan is your reality check—in fact, to make it more palatable, you may want to refer to it as your Reality Check Plan. Without said plan, it's easy to live in denial about your brilliant origami store or mime school bleeding you dry. Fleshing out a Reality Check Plan makes you own up to how much your office supplies and equipment will cost, how much you can expect to sell your first year, and how much revenue you need to make so you don't wind up living on Spam casserole for the rest of your life. Besides, if you do go the business-financing route, the bank won't even talk to you without a thoroughly hashed-out plan.

That said, if you're providing a service that doesn't require much overhead or start-up cash—say, as a freelance publicist or an event planner—a thirty-page Reality Check Plan is probably overkill. An abbreviated plan that pinpoints your goals, target market, possible specialties, rates, expenses, and projected revenue should do the trick.

Part of writing a business plan—er, a Reality Check Plan—is sizing up the competition: Are you going toe to toe against a leading

ANTI 9 to 5 tip

For business-plan templates or free start-up advice, see the SCORE, Counselors to America's Small Business, website at www.score.org. This nonprofit organization is the go-to resource for business newbies. Be sure to check out their information and training programs aimed at women and minorities, too. I can't stress enough how important it is to enlist the help of outside professionals like this when you don't know what you're doing. It may mean the difference between staying out of the cube and landing back in it a few years down the line.

computer-game conglomerate with tentacles in every major U.S. city, or a mom-and-pop geek shop across town? Is the market big enough to welcome one more gaming shop into the fray? What makes you stand out from the pack, anyway? Do you have a cool niche, perhaps computer games for technophobes?

You also need to determine the going rate for your type of service or product. "I had to really work the numbers to see how much I could charge—and how much the market would bear," says Erika Teschke, the legal eagle turned dog-walker. To do this, she grilled her own dog-walker and staked out other pet sitters in the dog park, inquiring about their rates and how long they'd been in business. Sometimes you can find how much the competition charges right on their website, or you can call them up and pose as a potential customer. You can consult an industry guide like *Photographer's Market*, or ask around at your professional association of choice. You want to charge enough so you can turn a profit, but not so much that you turn all potential customers away (especially if you're a newbie).

A word of caution: Government rules and regs prohibit price fixing—simply put, agreeing with other businesses on a set price for a product or service. For this reason, many web discussion lists and forums forbid questions of the "How much should I charge?" or "How much do you charge?" variety. Consider yourself warned.

ALWAYS BE CLOSING

In the movie *Glengarry Glen Ross,* Alec Baldwin plays an abusive motivational speaker who tries to psych up stumbling salesguys Jack Lemmon, Ed Harris, and Alan Arkin. "A-B-C: A, always, B, be, C, closing. Always be closing! Always be closing!" he barks at them, before dangling a pair of brass balls over his crotch. To land customers, I'm not suggesting you transmogrify into some fast-talking, Rolex-wearing sales hound who espouses bad, testosterone-laced metaphors. But I am suggesting you never rest on your laurels, never put all your eggs in one basket, and never commit any other sales cliché you can think of.

More than any other question, would-be fempreneurs ask me how I find my clients. When you are just starting out and hungry for work (or just plain hungry), tapping the people who already know and love you, from former employers to the current day gig you're leaving, makes sense. There's less of a learning curve for you and less for the "client" to explain. Nobody has to check anybody's references, and everybody wins.

Besides recycling former employers or hitting up family and friends, many small-business owners will tell you they get most of their customers by word of mouth. While no one's debating that a satisfied customer is the best form of advertising, your quest for clientele shouldn't begin and end with your referral list. It's far too easy to hunker down in your safe little comfort zone, letting only the same handful of clients know you're free every time your schedule clears up.

To ensure I bring in new blood from time to time, I like to keep a Customer Wish List. To make your own Customer Wish List, ask yourself, *If I could sell to any ten people or companies in the world, who would they be?* My favorite family-friendly Fortune 500? That hot new women-owned start-up I've been reading so much about? My town's answer to Melinda Gates? If you don't know, you once again have some recon to do.

Write this prospecting time into your weekly calendar so you don't blow it off. Call it something fun, like "Digging for Dollars." It may take a few months to land one of your dream customers; it may take a few years. But the better connected you are to other fempreneurs and industry players, the greater your odds are of being in the right place at the right time. When you do land one of your Top Ten, cross that customer off your list and add another in its place. The point is to always be striving for something more so your business doesn't grow stale and you don't get bored.

Know that potential customers will slam the door in your face or, worse, ignore your call or email entirely. The sooner you grow a thicker skin, the easier rejection will be. "I know a lot of women who are artists and writers and filmmakers, and they have a hard time telling themselves all the self-congratulatory things," says Blue Chevigny, thirty-four, an independent public-radio producer in New York. "I think you need a chorus on your shoulder, saying all the positive things everyone's ever said to you all the time."

Casting a wider net can help boost your confidence and cushion the blows: If I pitch five national magazine articles at once and three scoff at my idea but two bite, the not-a-snowball's-chance-in-hells don't sting quite so much. Keep a folder, scrapbook, or cigar box of any praise you receive for a job well done. This may sound like a hokey Stuart Smalley skit from *Saturday Night Live*, but during those lean, mean-old-world times, pulling out the client love letters to remind yourself that you're good enough, smart enough, and doggone it, people like you can keep you from drunk-dialing your former boss and asking for your job back.

ANTI 9 to 5 tip

Check out potential clients just as you would a future employer. When the web began to implode in 2000, I consulted other freelancers and the site FuckedCompany.com to find out if potential clients were going belly up. If your gut tells you the deal stinks, the deal stinks (even if the only things in your cupboards are cobwebs). There is such a thing as a hell client—for example, the stiffer who holds your payment hostage or the bloodsucker who makes 900 requests not covered in your contract. Working for a client from hell just eats up time you could have spent working for a more ethical, sane, paying customer.

Publicity on a dime

To turn your business into a household name, some shameless self-promotion is in order. Hopefully you've already printed up business cards and built a website. If not, get on it! Same goes for schooling everyone from your third cousin to your postal carrier about your upcoming art show or your freshly launched homebrew business. Relatives, especially moms and grandmothers, are like walking megaphones. So are like-minded freelancers, business owners, and craftivists. Never underestimate the power of the mouth.

But don't just play the telephone game and call it good. Herewith some low-budget tried-and-trues, culled from my many years of hustling for rent money and professional cred.

Flaunt your expertise. Online communities and discussion lists are perfect forums for helping others in your trade. Without hogging the floor, make your presence known by answering questions and providing links to articles, events, and resources you think would benefit the list. When you're recognized as an expert, word does travel.

Publish an e-newsletter. Once your business is hopping, email your contacts a monthly or quarterly update on what's new. Up to three short, fifty- to 200-word articles per issue do the trick. Include a table of contents at the top and an unsubscribe option at the bottom, and use spell-check.

Start a blog. Say you're an independent financial planner for Gen X and Gen Y women. And say you post at least a couple weekly tips or news items on paying off student loans or financing a car. Your clients, who already see you as a money maven, will relish your helpful posts and probably tell their friends to "check out this amazing money blog." If you're a blogging virgin, Blogger.com is a free and easy way to get started. And you can stay on top of industry headlines by having them emailed to you with Google alerts.

Donate goods or services. Annie Salafsky, co-owner of Helsing Junction Farm in Rochester, Washington, gets loads of recognition for the organic produce she donates to neighboring schools and agricultural events. Ditto for Searah, the Chicago sex-shop owner, who gives sex-ed talks to students at local colleges, social service agencies, and social groups. Not only is her community outreach work "really good PR" for her business, it also gives her another way to spread the sex-positive word.

🖉 *Partner up.* You know how all those aging rockers from the seventies do those tired summer stadium tours together? (Paging Don Henley.) That's because there's strength — and ticket sales — in numbers. I know you're still in your prime, but you're never too young to team up with other solo acts. Cohosting an exhibit, reading, launch party, or other type of open house with your fellow fempreneurs or freelanc-ers may draw a bigger crowd (and more media attention). Likewise, craftivist and artpreneur collectives, like BuyOlympia.com, can gener-ate more online hits than your lone website.

🖉 *Alert the media.* Anytime your business does something newsworthy — hosts a public bash, offers a unique class, makes a fat donation, gets a visit from Margaret Cho — it's a good opportunity to get some local press. Use the public library or the free advice on websites like PublicityInsider.com to learn how to write a press release, contact the media, and give a good interview. Look for opportunities to tie in to holidays and local events. Also, take advantage of the event calendars in your local papers to promote your in-store happenings. Either way, be sure to give them enough lead time (several weeks) so you don't miss their deadlines. And keep a camera handy in case The Notorious Cho does happen to waltz through your front door.

🖉 *Those who do, teach.* Do people always ask you how they can break into your field? Then consider offering yourself up to a professional association as a guest speaker. Or teach a class at a community cen-ter or facility you rent (a move that could earn you a bit of cash on the side). Just be sure you have your rap down before you walk into the classroom. You don't want to get caught with your proverbial pants down.

WHAT (NOT) TO CHARGE

I n her book *What to Charge: Pricing Strategies for Freelancers and Consultants,* Laurie Lewis lays out two rules for naming your price: Never quote a rate on the spot, and know your bottom line. I've found that clients love to ask, "So, what are your rates?" before clueing you in to what they need done. But that doesn't mean you have to answer on the spot. Get all the project details first, from the scope and deadline to the number of revisions expected and number of people you'll be working with. Then tell the client you'll get back to them with an estimate later in the day or the next morning.

Now off you go into your corner to figure out a fair price. Which brings us to Lewis' second rule: Know your bottom line—in other words, the lowest dollar amount you'd accept for this gig. To figure this out, break the project down into steps, from the hours you'll spend poring over research materials right down to that final double-check of your work. Next, keeping in mind the going market rate for this type of project (in your client's particular industry), ask yourself what the minimum hourly rate you'd do this project for is. If you want to quote the client a flat fee, multiply your minimum hourly rate by the amount of hours you anticipate the project taking.

Ready for the fun part? Take a deep breath, my freelance friends, because it's time to haggle. Don't ask for that minimum hourly rate or flat fee you hashed out in the previous paragraph. Ask for a little more, a figure that's maybe 5 or 10 percent higher. That way, if the client tries to talk you down, you're not starting at your "I won't do it for less" price. And if you foresee big fat expenses on this project, ask to have those covered, too.

That said, if you're a newbie looking to flesh out a skimpy portfolio, taking a few gigs for less than your "I won't do it for less" fee, and even doing a couple freebies, is a good way to build up experience. I certainly did my share of discount jobs and pro bono gigs (freebies) to beef up my writing samples back in the day. Just don't give too much away.

Once you and your client agree on the price, put it in writing. If your client works regularly with freelancers, they'll probably send you a standard contract. But even an informal email outlining what tasks you'll do, when project milestones are due, what the rate is and when you'll get paid, what expenses you'll recoup, and how many rounds of revisions you'll do (I suggest just one) can do the trick. Don't sign contracts blindly. If you don't understand a contract, consult a free-lance pal who knows more than you do, or your friendly SCORE counselor, or professional organizations like the National Writers Union or Graphic Artists Guild, which offer free contract advice

ANTI 9 to 5 tip

People always ask if I charge my clients for meetings. The answer is yes and no. I'm perfectly happy to do the complimentary one-hour "getting to know you" meeting, be it at the client's office, on the phone, or over email. Besides gathering all the necessary info, this preliminary powwow lets me show the client my portfolio and offer a couple suggestions so they can see what I'm made of—something like, "This web copy might pack more of a punch if the sentences weren't each ten lines long." Beware the prospective client who asks you to four preliminary meetings before you even agree on a rate. Unless it's a big, multimonth project, like writing a book or developing a clothing line or drafting mechanicals for a shopping mall, one free meeting should do the trick. All others should be on the clock.

to members. And think twice before you sign anything that says you cannot work for the client's competitors (which is known as a "non-compete clause").

Know that negotiating rates and contracts takes practice. It may sound daunting now, but trust me, you'll get better at it with time. And the more seasoned entrepreneurs you glean tips from, the better equipped you'll be to haggle without batting an eye.

SHOW ME THE MONEY

Once you've researched how much your business's start-up expenses will run you (and channeled your inner haggler), you need to figure out how you'll finance it. Brett saved the $20,000 she needed to launch her clothing line, Borne, by dog-sitting and house-sitting for eight months, on top of working her day job. Maggie, of Supermaggie, put several hundred dollars' worth of craft supplies on her credit card to start her business because she didn't have much savings. (She figured telling the bank, "Hi, I'd like to make handmade felt scarves. Can I have a loan, please?" wouldn't fly.) But Maggie was careful to pay off her credit card as soon as she made back the money in sales, and to reinvest any extra money from her 9-to-5 paycheck in her business.

The Small Business Administration (SBA) also features programs for more sizable loans, and some state loan programs offer women and minority business owners lower interest rates through commercial banks. But, like credit card financing, borrowing money can wind up biting you in the ass if your business flops. And as Sharon Miller of the Renaissance Entrepreneurship Center points out, "If your business does fail, you might owe $50,000 in a loan, on top of everything." Makes saving your pennies and starting small sound more and more appealing, right?

While there's no such thing as a for-profit business grant (despite what the late-night infomercials would have you believe), you may be eligible for a microloan (up to $35,000) through the SBA or one of the hundreds of microenterprise organizations throughout the country. For more information, check out the "Must-See Resources" appendix.

ANTI 9-TO-5 ACTION PLAN

This action plan breaks the business of starting your own solo venture into more digestible chunks. Depending on how much time and money you have to devote to your shiny new solo project, you may be spreading this action plan out over a few months or a couple years. Whether you plan to moonlight or dive into business ownership whole hog, the important thing is to start taking some baby steps now.

STAGE 1: STUDY UP	
Start date	Checklist
	Start attending the monthly meetings of at least one professional association for women entrepreneurs.
	Pick the brain of at least one seasoned business owner a week.
	Take a business-planning class or talk to an advisor at an association like SCORE, Counselors to America's Small Business.

STAGE 2: THINK LIKE AN MBA	
Start date	Checklist
	Do the market research to see if people will buy what you're selling, what the going rate is, and who your competitors are.
	Crunch the numbers to see how much starting and running the business will cost, and how much more cash you need.
	Write your Reality Check Plan, including the fees you'll charge.

STAGE 3: MAP YOUR ESCAPE ROUTE	
Start date	Checklist
	Decide how much longer to stay at your day job to stockpile the industry know-how and savings you need to start your business.
	If planning to line up part-time, flex, temp, or bread-and-butter freelance work to subsidize your business, start making these contacts now.
	Talk with an accountant or financial advisor if you're at all hazy about how going solo will affect your personal income.

STAGE 4: OPEN YOUR DOORS	
Start date	Checklist
	Write your Customer Wish List and spend at least a morning a week digging for dollars (prospecting).
	Announce your grand opening. Or throw a launch party at your studio, storefront, or favorite café.
	Read a book or website on how to work the media, or have your PR-savvy friend give you a crash course.

chapter 7

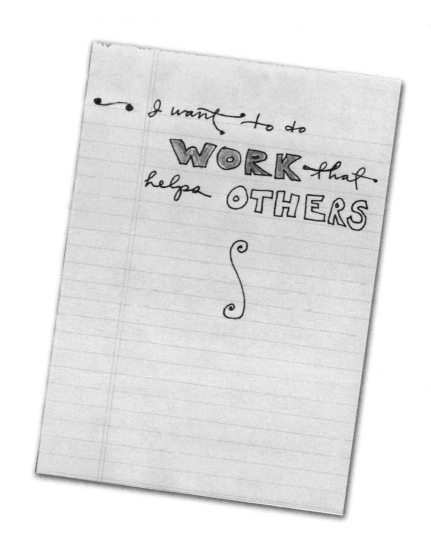

I want to do
WORK that
helps **OTHERS**

"Isn't it funny how some people go out of their way

to help others, when others just fire them?"

—Julia Roberts in *Erin Brockovich*, 2000

You've heard the story a hundred times: Some overworked exec has a life-changing moment, quits her job, and goes all Angelina Jolie—wanting, commendably, to save starving babies, Third World populations, and anything else in her path. Lisa Fitzhugh had that moment early on in life. Raised by an artsy single mom who lived hand to mouth, Lisa went the overachiever route in school and then fleshed out her resume with a series of super-stable jobs in the political arena. She saw politics as a way to effect change in the world while making a solid living.

At age thirty, Lisa was tapped to work as a senior environmental aide for the Seattle mayor, an incredibly high-profile gig, especially for someone so young. The job was all consuming, the pay fantastic, the prestige as high as it gets. An "intense workaholic" at the time, she regularly put in eighty-hour weeks without batting an eye.

Lisa's life-altering moment happened a year into the gig working for the mayor, when she was diagnosed with breast cancer at age thirty-one. The tumor was aggressive and called for ultra-rigorous treatments. "It sent my world into a tailspin," she says. But instead of taking a leave from her job to combat the disease, Lisa kept working while undergoing chemo and radiation because, as she puts it, "I was such a control freak."

After a year of treatments, Lisa made a full recovery. But emotionally, all was not well. Thoughts like, *Oh my god, I have no inner life* began to plague her. She couldn't shake the nagging feeling she should be doing something more important. So she resigned from the mayor's office and began researching the viability of starting an after-school arts education program for at-risk kids. "I must have been 'channeling,' or something," Lisa says, because she had absolutely no experience in arts education. But immersing herself in the creative world became her way to heal her heart and head after the cancer.

In spring 2000, with the help of a friend savvy in all things nonprofit and the financial support of her boyfriend, Lisa began fleshing out her idea. Meetings with community leaders, educators, lawyers, and financiers ensued. Her thick Rolodex and political know-how proved invaluable, especially since artsy-fartsy, liberal Seattle has one of the highest concentrations of nonprofits in the country (meaning less handouts to go around). Just half a year later, in fall 2000, Arts Corps opened its doors and held its first handful of after-school classes at six different community centers.

By the time I interviewed Lisa, she was thirty-eight and cancer free. Arts Corps was six years old and had grown to eight times its original size, providing thirty Seattle facilities with fifty classes per quarter on everything from hip-hop and spoken word to Brazilian dance and digital photography, all taught by professional artists. The organization, which runs on a $1 million budget, now fetches huge, multiyear grants from places like the Gates Foundation, and demand for its classes far exceeds the organization's ability to supply them. But that's not to say it's been easy. Lisa worked without pay that first year until Arts Corps landed a couple of substantial grants. "It took flesh and blood to get this thing off the ground," including working around the clock for months on end, she says. Happily, this is one job that's been a labor of love for her.

I know what some of you are thinking: *Yep, that Lisa's inspiring, but I don't have a fat bank account, contacts at City Hall, sixty spare hours a week, and a domestic partner to carry me financially while I set off to save the world.* Not to worry. Most women don't. That's why in this chapter you'll hear from women who've found alternate ways to get a grassroots program off the ground, be it raising money for domestic violence or teaching yoga to homeless teens or championing the rights of women in Mongolia (many of these programs hail from Seattle, since I'm most familiar with my local nonprofit landscape). Or maybe, like me, your do-gooder goals are less lofty. Maybe instead of running the social-service show, you want to transition from your soulless corporate job to a meaningful one in the nonprofit sector (perhaps one with more flexible hours). Or maybe you're looking to land the volunteer gig of your dreams. This chapter will give you ideas on those fronts, too.

So, ready to roll up your sleeves and make your little corner of the globe a better place?

ON KISSING THE FOR-PROFIT WORLD GOODBYE

"My life in the corporate world was at times very satisfying, and was certainly more lucrative, but it never gave me goose bumps or the same thrill I get now," says Gwynn Cassidy, thirty-five, cofounder of Girls in Government, a nonprofit organization in New York that encourages girls to become political leaders. Gwynn is one of many women I talked to who left the for-profit workforce to chase that save-the-world high at a job in the nonprofit sector. (Gwynn also works part-time for the National Organization for Women.) In her former 9-to-5 life, Gwynn was paid to wax poetic about the merits of mascara and zit cream at a major media conglomerate. Her work now, encouraging more girls to wake up in the morning and say, "I want to be president," couldn't be more of a 180.

Of course, Gwynn didn't go from espousing the virtues of Botox to empowering young women overnight. A fair amount of scrimping, saving, schmoozing, volunteering, fact-finding, and dues-paying at nonprofit jobs took place. To deal with her anticipated dip in income, she took several months' worth of freelance work on top of her day job, stowed all her earnings in a savings account, hid away her credit cards, and put a moratorium on shopping for all nonessentials.

Expect to encounter similar hurdles on the road to becoming a nonprofit superstar. So before you start looking for nonprofit job openings, take the time to figure out what cause gives you those goose bumps Gwynn mentioned. Do you want to protect the whales, the artists, abortion rights, or your local bike trails? Do you want to help immigrants get on their feet, homeless women land jobs, or kids learn to read? Take it from someone who's counseled umpteen friends disgruntled by nonprofit work they couldn't rally behind: If you sign up to champion an issue that doesn't blow your skirt up, you'll soon find yourself in the same soul-quashing boat you were in at your corporate gig.

Your next order of business should be to volunteer, volunteer, volunteer, and then volunteer some more. Considering the U.S. Bureau of Labor Statistics reports that one in three women volunteer in this country (compared with one in four men—hmm), you'd best do your part to keep up if you want that fabulous new nonprofit gig.

"Nothing should be 'beneath' you," says Janet Boguch of Non-Profit Works, a nonprofit-management consulting firm. "If you are interested in the arts, consider being a volunteer usher or selling refreshments at different theaters. If you are interested in social services, consider bagging food at the food bank." That way, when you write your heartfelt cover letters and plead your case at interviews about why you want to change fields, the hiring managers will see you mean business.

Get as wide a range of experience in the nonprofit trenches as you can, too—from fundraising to programming to event planning. "Be a sponge and just jump forward to every opportunity," says Whitney Smith, thirty-four, the founder and co-CEO of Girls For A Change, a nonprofit organization that teaches low-income girls in California to work for social change. "The leaders at nonprofits get really excited about young people who are jazzed and want to make change. You can really move up quickly if you put your mind to it."

Since far too many nonprofits are run on shoestring budgets by people with much more passion than business sense, be sure you do the necessary detective work we talked about earlier in the book. Make sure you're working for an outfit with an actual revenue stream. The free website GuideStar.org lets you view charities' IRS filings (forms known as 990s) and will even walk you through deciphering the documents. But don't stop at an organization's finances. Sniff out where you'll be working, and with whom. Way back when, in her less savvy days, nonprofit consultant Janet Boguch accepted a job offer at what she thought was her dream organization, only to find herself working alone each day at a cardboard table in a frigid attic with no heat. Not exactly a dream come true. As Seattle nonprofit veteran Lynn Stromski, thirty-three, warns, "Do everything you can to make sure you're not walking into a minefield."

PICK THE PLUM VOLUNTEER GIG

Maybe you're trying to beef up your nonprofit experience to impress that hotshot downtown foundation you want to work at. Or maybe you don't want to change jobs at all but want to volunteer on the side—which, I can attest, can definitely distract you from the pain of an onerous day gig. Before you sign up to help out, though, familiarize yourself with the lay of the nonprofit land in your community. Check out the arts and social service organizations written up and advertised in your alt weekly newspapers, and check out sites like VolunteerMatch.org and Idealist.org to see what unpaid gigs exist.

I know I just paid some lip service to not turning up your nose at the crappier volunteer chores if those are what you're handed. After all, *someone* has to stuff those Planned Parenthood envelopes. But that doesn't mean you should rush blindly into any volunteer gig without getting all the facts first—from the job description to the orientation process to the commitment expected. And don't be guilted into saying yes when you really mean no or "Let me think about it." You're not doing anyone any favors if you over-commit and wind up ditching your volunteer shifts. As my nonprofit pals attest, having to "clean up" after a flaky volunteer is worse than having no help at all.

That said, don't let your "back-office suck-up" phase drag on forever. Be proactive. Let the volunteer coordinator know of any unique skill you possess from the get-go, whether it's translating, database programming, proofreading, accounting, or animal whispering. After you've proven you can wield a letter opener, remind her of your talents outside of dodging paper cuts and ask for more challenging work.

Here's an example: My friend Rosemary, a former book editor, took a volunteer gig as a jill-of-all-trades at an abortion clinic in her late twenties. The only job requirement was a clean background check. Besides honing her reception skills, the clinic gig gave her hands-on experience in counseling women about reproductive issues. "It was tough, because I was working full-time Monday through Friday, and I was working every Saturday at the clinic," she says. But it was worth it: "I was so inspired by the work, and I felt so bored at my editing job." Within a year, a salaried office-manager position opened up at the clinic, and Rosemary leapt at the opportunity. That was in 1996. Rosemary has since gone on to become a licensed social worker whose book-publishing days are a distant memory.

If you're *not* trying to score a paid gig in the nonprofit sector (and thus don't need to impress anyone with your envelope-stuffing prowess), I say push for more hands-on volunteer work. I've certainly always gotten more out of walking dogs at the animal shelter, working a domestic violence hotline, and joining an event-planning committee than I have out of pushing papers. I already do enough of that in my paid gig.

If you have a computer and an Internet connection, don't overlook volunteering virtually for organizations in your neck of the woods or other states—a great option for those with limited time, transportation, or a disability that makes commuting tough. More and more nonprofit organizations are using volunteers who telecommute. Alliance for International Women's Rights, a New York–based organization that helps women's groups in Central Asia, is one such outfit. Founder Lisa Herb, thirty-nine, who does much of the organization's work from her own home, maintains a stable of armchair volunteers who provide editing, research, web maintenance, and advice on women's rights to female advocacy groups in Mongolia and Kazakhstan.

CREATE YOUR OWN GRASSROOTS GIG

In *Grassroots: A Field Guide for Feminist Activism,* coauthors Jennifer Baumgardner and Amy Richards write that activism isn't just for "people who chain themselves to trees or ruin dinner by lecturing their families and friends about factory farming." Besides calling your congressperson, donating money, or volunteering—which Baumgardner and Richards label "The Generic Three"—what can you do to make an impact on the causes near and dear to your heart?

I talked to a number of women who take a sky's-the-limit approach to practicing not-so-random acts of activism. Many are fans of running marathons to raise money, campaigning for their favorite politicians, and taking a volunteer vacation (covered in the next chapter). Here are some of their other top suggestions.

Host a house party. My friend Valerie, ever the social networker and educator, has a talent for putting together informational salons. She'll invite over a few dozen friends, whom she'll treat to drinks, snacks, literature, a speaker or two, and an insightful political discussion. Over the years her salons have taught me about everything from the World Trade Organization to the Homeland Security Act to the ongoing endangerment of Roe v. Wade.

Besides educating your pals about your pet cause, house parties are a fantastic way to raise dollars for your favorite charity or arts organization. Invite a couple dozen friends, ask each to bring a guest, and suggest a reasonable donation. People will often meet it, if not give more. You may even want to plant a friend to say, "Hey, I want to give $100 to help the animals," suggests Whitney Smith, founder and co-CEO of Girls For A Change. After all, what's a little healthy competition among friends with their wallets out?

Mine the web. Never underestimate the power of your computer (or one you borrow at the library). Think about it: How many times have you signed a petition, written your congressperson, or given money online when an organization like MoveOn.org or your favorite politician came calling through cyberspace?

"You can start your own movement, you can blog about issues important to you, you can educate yourself, you can tutor a child, you can build a website that extols the virtues of getting more women in elected office," says Gwynn of Girls in Government, which in 2006 launched TheREALHot100.org, a send-up of *Maxim*'s annual "Hot 100" list that lauds young women not for their bodies, but because they're smart, outspoken, and politically active.

Get on board. Joining a nonprofit board of directors is a giant responsibility. So why do it? For one thing, it's a cool resume-booster, whether you're trying to make inroads in the nonprofit management world or another field. For another thing, as Amy Wheeler, executive director of Hedgebrook, a women's writing retreat in the Pacific Northwest, says, it's a way artists and activists can help shape the future of organizations they care deeply about. (Amy was a Hedgebrook writer-in-residence turned board president before becoming the retreat's head honcho.)

Since serving on a board is like volunteering on steroids, passion for and serious knowledge about the cause is a must, as are the time and willingness to roll up your sleeves and do the heavy lifting. Sure, being a fundraising fiend with a knack for networking and shameless promotion helps, but many nonprofit boards are equally tickled to tap any legal, leadership, accounting, administrative, or business management skills people have. Before you commit, be sure to Google past and current board members (usually listed on the organization's website) to look for any red flags.

If you're not quite board material yet but you'd like to be, volunteer with the organization first to learn the ropes. Consider taking a workshop in board management through an organization like the United Way, and check out the additional resources in the "Must-See Resources" appendix.

Team up with bigger fish. My friend Terry, a technical editor who teaches yoga on the side, wanted to bring her classes to disadvantaged women and teens who couldn't afford Seattle's yoga-studio prices, much less the color-coordinated yoga pants and tank tops. By teaming up with Street Yoga, a West Coast organization that serves homeless and at-risk teens, Terry was able to persuade a local homeless women's shelter and a health clinic to provide class space. What's more, she wrangled a handful of other yoga instructors to help her teach the weekly classes.

And by joining Eve Ensler's global V-Day movement in 1999, Kirsten Johnson and five friends were able to coproduce performances of *The Vagina Monologues* on several Minnesota college campuses. By 2006, their incarnation of the annual production had raised $80,000 for Minnesota women's shelters and advocacy groups. (And this is just the tip of the iceberg. In 2005 alone, volunteers around the world threw more than 2,500 V-Day benefits, and in its first eight years, the V-Day movement raised $30 million to stop violence against women and girls and educated millions about abuse. To get involved, go to www.vday.org.)

Get your day job in on the act. Maybe you can't think of too many redeeming things about your current day gig, other than the fact that it keeps your phone turned on. Getting your coworkers to pony up cash, holiday gifts, or food for underprivileged kids might make you feel otherwise. How do you convince the big cheese to support the little guy or gal? If you work at a sizable company, talk to your community relations or human resources department—they eat this up, Whitney says. Because it's good PR for the company, they'll likely be willing to help you with the planning and promotion. If you work at a small company, talk with your boss or whoever manages the company's public image.

ANTI 9 to 5 tip

In the summer of 2006, Los Angeles's Animal Services agency, tasked with putting an end to euthanasia, pissed off half of City Hall by agreeing to accept donations raised by a bikini contest held at a local Hooters restaurant. The fundraiser name? "Hooters for Neuters." While I'm not suggesting you'd do anything quite so retro, this gaffe shows why you need the green light from all involved parties before you agree to raise money—from business sponsors (say, your employer) to the nonprofit receiving the donations. Ditto for collecting wish-list items, such as winter jackets for a women's homeless shelter. So before you start advertising your house party or office clothing drive, get your beneficiary's blessing, ask if they have any particular fundraising rules you need to follow (they may), and make sure they actually need those winter coats.

But before you speak up, think about how the program you're suggesting will benefit the company. See if other businesses have started a similar recycling, financial matching, or mentoring program and find out how it's impacted them: Has it raised employee morale? Earned the company some positive press? Get coworkers on board so the powers that be know staff will support the program. Put all this in writing, along with *how* you plan to implement the program, and include any relevant websites, articles, or statistics you find so people see you mean business.

SO YOU WANT TO START A NONPROFIT?

S tarting a nonprofit organization is a lot like starting a for-profit business—you need a serious dose of passion, moxie, and business savvy. One big difference: With a nonprofit, you have to ask for money every step of the way. But before you can hold your hand out, you need to nail down the market research, business plan, and tireless schmoozing we talked about in Chapter 6. You also need to get legit from the get-go, filing the proper legal docs and tax forms, as you'll see momentarily—all of which cost money.

Like Arts Corps Executive Director Lisa Fitzhugh said earlier in this chapter, founding a nonprofit organization is a gigantic undertaking, so you'll definitely want to school yourself before you leap. The "Must-See Resources" section in the appendix includes references and websites that can get you started. Many local nonprofit assistance centers offer classes and resources that can help, too.

Even if you start the organization on the side or split the lion's share of duties with a business partner, you're still in for a load of legwork. To see if you're up to the task, check out what seasoned nonprofit founders and directors say getting a program off the ground entails. Then have yourself a good long think and check all items on the list you're game for taking on.

❏ *Avoid doubling up.* The point is to serve some unmet need in your community, not reinvent the wheel. With roughly 1.5 million nonprofit organizations in this country, the last thing you want to do is compete with an existing nonprofit for precious donor dollars or volunteer hours. Home Alive, a Seattle organization, is one of my favorite examples of a nonprofit providing a community service that was sorely lacking. The program started in 1993, after Seattle musician Mia Zapata was raped and strangled on her way home from a neighborhood bar (a murder unsolved for a decade). Intent on turning their grief on its head, nine of Mia's artist and musician friends raised money through benefit performances and CD sales and began offering affordable self-defense classes in the community. As I write this in 2006, Home Alive is a national go-to resource for antiviolence education and safety training.

To see if the program you're proposing fills an untapped niche, talk to your target population's advocates, including community leaders, teachers, politicians, and other nonprofit groups. All this is, of course, fodder for your business plan. Don't be afraid to emulate a social-service idea that's working in another geographic location but is missing from your neck of the woods. A friend of mine in Seattle started The Ruby Room, an organization that provides free gowns to underprivileged prom-bound girls, after researching (and seeing Oprah profile) a similar Chicago organization, The Glass Slipper Project. And the founders of Just Cauz, a Seattle organization that raises money for underprivileged kids by hosting happy hours for twenty-and thirtysomethings, modeled their organization after similar groups in Chicago and Washington, D.C.

❏ *Rally the troops.* It's not enough to poll community members during your fact-finding phase. Throughout your nonprofit's life, you'll have to sell everyone from City Hall to your former boss on your mission (which you of course shouldn't do till you know your MO backwards and forwards). If you can't do this, don't expect anyone to whip out their checkbook. The more confident, convincing, and articulate you are, the more community support you'll drum up.

To get more comfortable speaking before groups of two, ten, or fifty, practice your rap in front of friends who can give you feedback. If you're public-speaking challenged, take a class or sign up for a structured public-speaking club, like Toastmasters. (Yes, I've actually done a public-speaking class, even allowed myself to be videotaped. Once you get past the initial trauma, it *does* help.)

❑ *Master the ask.* "I feel like I got a master's degree in asking people for things this year," Gwynn of Girls in Government says. "I've definitely grown some balls." Like Gwynn, you have to get used to tapping people and businesses to donate their time, money, goods, sponsorship, real estate, and professional skills. And I do mean all people—from your mom to your mail carrier. Because if you're not related to Warren Buffett, no one's going to hand you the ideas, contacts, and cash you need to run your organization just for the heck of it. The worst that can happen is that they say no.

❑ *Sweat the legal and financial stuff.* Unless you are a lawyer, you need one in your court. By law, your venture can't do much of anything (accept donations, apply for grants, provide services) until you incorporate the organization and apply for tax exemption with the IRS. If I've already lost you, not to worry. Securing an attorney to see you through the legal rigmarole of starting and running a nonprofit isn't too tough. Many firms take on pro bono clients (clients they do freebies for). After all, it makes them look good. All you have to do is ask, and ask you should: Whitney Smith estimates landing a lawyer to sit on her board saved Girls For A Change $15,000 in start-up costs.

Cozying up to folks who know a thing or two about nonprofit accounting, business development, and grant writing is another must. Remember, you'll soon be filing tax forms, managing budgets, and asking the government and various foundations for money. And whatever you do, don't put off or blow off dealing with any legal or tax matters. "This is serious stuff," Gwynn says. "You can't just stick your head in the sand." If you don't understand a document the IRS mails you, ask those in the know to translate it into plain English for you.

❑ *Delegate your heart out.* "Don't be afraid to hire people or get volunteers who know more than you do," says Whitney. The idea is to use your resources wisely, including your own energy and time. You can't do it all, so surround yourself with people passionate about your mission and choose wisely, because you'll be working closely with these folks. Managing volunteers and recruiting your board of directors is an art. Take advantage of the online FAQs and classes on these aspects of nonprofit management offered by your regional nonprofit assistance center. Many community colleges also offer courses in running a social enterprise.

If any of these duties fall outside your comfort zone, make sure you team up with partners, advisors, and board members whose talents pick up where yours leave off. If most of the items in this list sound positively godawful to you, you're better off exploring some of the chapter's other suggestions.

WHEN SOCIAL SERVICE MEETS COMMERCE

One thing you hear over and over in nonprofit circles is how multiple sources of funding can increase your organization's life expectancy—from private donations, grants, and fundraising events to bona fide earned income. It's pretty much the same "Don't put all your eggs in one basket" principle that small-business owners

151

The fine art of throwing a fundraiser

Since my biggest fundraising effort to date is the hundred bucks I raised selling Girl Scout cookies as a kid, I asked some fundraising pros for their top tips. It doesn't matter what you've got cooking—a house party, pancake breakfast, silent auction, poetry reading, rock show, or race for charity. When it comes to raising money, say these vets, you'll learn the most from your mistakes. But to boost your learning curve, they agreed to offer up some of their hard-won wisdom here.

"Fundraising benefits are fantastic as an outreach method," says Lynn Stromski, the nonprofit vet you met earlier. "It's called *friend-raising.*" Having a goal in mind other than raking in lucre is optimum. Throwing a fundraiser is a ton of work—it can take up to a year to plan a large-scale event like an auction—and since there's no guarantee you'll meet your target financial goal, you might as well milk the fact that you've gathered a roomful of people for all it's worth. Use the event to entice new community advocates and volunteers, distribute literature, influence people's political vote, or generate publicity. (If you're not much for media relations, enlist a friend who is. Also see the "Publicity on a Dime" sidebar in Chapter 6, as well as books like Jason Salzman's *Making the News: A Guide for Activists and Nonprofits.*)

When brainstorming event ideas, think about who your target donors are, what they can afford, and what they like to do. Seattle fundraising

---

live and die by. If one of your cash cows buys the farm, you're not set out to pasture, too.

"Grantors love to see earned income," says Lynn Stromski, who in the past decade has worn such hats as nonprofit board member, research manager, and executive director. As you can imagine, money people pay in exchange for a product or service can be easier to predict and less likely to fluctuate than grants you apply for (and pray you receive).

Bike Works, another grassroots legend in Seattle, runs a bicycle repair shop and offers classes that bring in more than half its annual community programs budget—a huge boon for a nonprofit. Besides group Just Cauz suggests a cover charge of ten bucks for the happy-hour parties they throw for Gen X and Y cube monkeys. "I am the perfect face for who Just Cauz is targeting," says Sarah Armstrong, thirty-one, one of twelve friends who comprise the organization's board of directors. Like most people under age thirty-five who work for a living, Sarah is far more likely to attend an event with a nominal, *optional* cover charge than to go to some $250 black-tie gala. Obviously, the strategy's working: On average, the group's happy hours have drawn about 200 people and raised about $3,000 per night.

Be considerate of your guests, advise Baumgardner and Richards, the authors of *Grassroots*. Keep the agenda short and sweet, limit your remarks to fifteen minutes, and answer a few questions. Then point your audience toward your (very succinct) literature or those T-shirts you're selling. Be mindful not to bore your audience or keep them up past their bedtime. And by all means, work the room. Nobody appreciates a bunch of hosts who hide in the corner, chatting amongst themselves.

One more thing: Follow up *promptly* after the event with a personalized thank you note. Even better if you can let your donors know how their contribution helped, whether it meant buying a new computer for the local Boys & Girls Club or paying the printing costs for your literary zine's next four issues. The more personal the touch, the stronger the connection.

recycling old bikes and promoting two wheel transportation in the community (instead of gas guzzling), the organization provides adult mentorship and bike-repair instruction to low-income kids, who, in return for time spent fixing up old bikes, earn a cycle they couldn't otherwise afford. In the past decade, the group has also donated hundreds of bikes to local nonprofit organizations that serve disadvantaged populations, and has sent about 2,000 bikes to villages in Ghana.

You don't have to run a nonprofit business to be a socialpreneur, however. Take Chimène Cadeau. Since 2004, the thirty-five-year-old Phoenix resident has been running a small coffee shop—called

CommUnity Market—where she exclusively brews Café Femenino, a Fair Trade Organic (FTO) coffee harvested and produced by a women's foundation in a Peruvian village. Although she could make more money by selling non-FTO coffee, Chimène and her customers choose to support the businesses of South American farming women and their families (who, without the FTO program, would get a pretty crappy wage).

Moral of the story: Study how other non- and for-profits you admire bring in the bucks. Soak up the wisdom of social enterprise organizations, books, and websites. Innovation is the name of the game. There's no one right way to run the social-service show.

SHOW ME THE MONEY

Besides asking everyone you know for the moon, perhaps the easiest way to finance a grassroots project is to pitch it to an existing organization and have it run under their umbrella, as my friend Terry did when she started a program teaching yoga to homeless kids and women. Ditto for jumping on board an existing grassroots campaign like V-Day, as Kirsten Johnson did.

If you can't afford the incorporation fees needed to start a non-profit but you're hell-bent on starting a program of your own, finding a fiscal sponsor (a.k.a. a fiscal agent) may be your best bet. According to *Nonprofit Kit for Dummies,* "In this approach, your new project becomes a sponsored program of an existing nonprofit organization. Contributions earmarked for your project are tax deductible because they're made to the sponsoring agency." Or, as Gwynn Cassidy of Girls in Government translates, "When someone wants to be able to write us a big fat check and write it off [for tax purposes], they'll be able to write it to our fiscal agent, and the fiscal agent cuts us a check."

Having a larger organization handle your accounting like this not only saves you start-up hours and costs, but also lets you focus on getting your program up and running. So how do you get a fiscal sponsor? You do your homework, find an established organization in your neck of the woods with a mission related to yours, show them your business plan, and plead your case (Gwynn uses Legal Momentum, a legal and policy advocacy group for women, as the fiscal sponsor of Girls in Government). If you're stumped, talk to your local community foundation for suggestions. Know that some fiscal sponsors will often take a fee—5 to 15 percent, says the *Nonprofit Kit for Dummies*. And you'll want to sign a contract agreement, samples of which you can find on the web.

If you want to cut out the middleman, running your organization on the side while maintaining other work (like contract attorney Lisa Herb, who uses the web to champion women's rights in Mongolia) enables you to continue eating while getting your program off the ground. Even so, Lisa poured about $10,000 of her own money into her venture's start-up costs, so consider yourself warned. Before you dive in, cost out your expenses and make sure you have—or can raise—the start-up capital. If you need a refresher on this, see the previous chapter.

ANTI 9-TO-5 ACTION PLAN

As you may have guessed, many of the topics in this chapter could fill an entire book. So before you bulldoze in, educate thyself. The "Must-See Resources" and "Boss in a Box" sections in the appendix can get you started.

Depending on how big a bite of the community-activism pie you want to take—be it volunteering twenty hours a month, sitting on a board of directors, or starting a full-fledged nonprofit organization—you may spread out this plan over several weeks, several months, or a couple of years. And depending on how high you want to climb the social-service totem pole, some of the stages may not apply to you.

STAGE 1: GET THE LAY OF THE NONPROFIT LAND	
Start date	Checklist
	Figure out what cause you want to champion—be it the arts, the environment, social justice, child welfare, or getting decent politicians in office.
	Take stock of your specialized skills, and revise your resume as needed.
	Make a list of the top five organizations or visionaries you want to work with.

STAGE 2: COZY UP TO YOUR DREAM ORG	
Start date	Checklist
	Start sleuthing and schmoozing. Collect as much dirt on your paid or unpaid dream organization—from the effectiveness of its board to the feasibility of its fundraising goals.
	Push yourself to work in a new role or environment. If you usually camp out at a computer monitor, try mentoring others, working outdoors, or doing manual labor.
	Remind your supervisor of your unique talents and volunteer to help with additional projects.
	Extra credit: Sign up for a nonprofit-management class.

STAGE 3: MOVE UP THE SOCIAL-SERVICE LADDER	
Start date	Checklist
	Collect experience in at least three avenues of running a nonprofit—for example, volunteer coordination, community outreach, and budget management.
	Get on the planning committee of a fundraising event so you can see how it's done.
	Extra credit: Throw a one-off benefit or house party. Be sure to work with the beneficiary on handling promotions and donations.
	Extra credit: Start a social-service program under the umbrella of your employer or an existing nonprofit.
	Extra credit: Commit your time and energy to a nonprofit board of directors.

STAGE 4: START YOUR OWN GRASSROOTS GROUP	
Start date	Checklist
	Research the need, fine-tune your MO, and write up your business plan.
	Rally as much community support as you can for your pet program.
	Troll for donations (cash and material), partners, volunteers, and anything else you need.
	Get a pro bono attorney, financial whiz, and business maven in your corner. File the necessary legal paperwork.
	Figure out how you'll deal with the accounting—through a fiscal sponsor or by your lonesome.

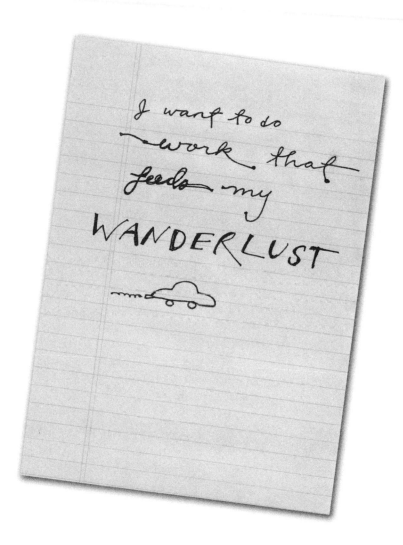

chapter 8

I want to do ~~work~~ that ~~feeds~~ my WANDERLUST

"When you have begun to feel at home in the out-of-doors on

hikes and treasure hunts, you will want to have a real camping trip.

This is quite different from planning a party at home.

It takes even more careful thought ahead of time. . . . "

—From *Book of the Camp Fire Girls*, 1962

Traci Macnamara is one of those enviable people who doesn't have a permanent address because she's always working somewhere fabulous. When I met the thirty-year-old Washington native, she had just finished her second stretch working at McMurdo Station, the largest U.S. station for scientific research in Antarctica. Her job there? To radio scientists at remote field camps each day to see if they were still among the living and needed any supplies. This was a step up from Traci's first McMurdo contract as a general assistant (GA), which is a glorified way of saying "she who spends summer (high temperature: 30 degrees Fahrenheit) clad in Carhartts and super-insulated moon boots, shoveling ice, and delivering fuel to scientists twelve hours a day."

"It was such a crap job," Traci says of her initial GA contract at the continent's largest science station. "I mean, it was dirty and nasty." And yet this former English professor found life at McMurdo heavenly, so much so that she stayed on through Antarctica's bitter winter (-100 degrees Fahrenheit with the wind chill—meaning no going outside whatsoever) and has since returned to the continent for a second multimonth stint.

You're probably wondering what prompted a gainfully employed academic to head off to the tundra in the first place. Let's just say that at age twenty-seven, she needed a fresh start—and we're talking the "anything goes" kind. At the time, she was living in Colorado Springs, where she'd been teaching and married for two years. But the work wasn't satisfying, her marriage was on the outs, and her world was, as they say, crumbling. So when a handful of cycling pals applied for entry-level gigs at McMurdo, Traci gave the application a spin too, despite her hunch that she "wasn't even qualified to be a dishwasher." But entry-level is entry-level, and soon she was off to Antarctica for ten straight life-altering months.

What does Traci love about working at McMurdo? Everything. The other free spirits, outdoor buffs, and globe-trotters she swings her shovel alongside. The fact that at the end of the day, her mind isn't swirling with deadlines, lesson plans, and university politics. (Instead, "you just put your shovel up and you're done.") The impressive chunk of change she amasses by the end of each contract. Running at dawn against the backdrop of snowcapped peaks, skate-skiing after work across pristine ice shelves, landing special assignments on U.S. Coast Guard ships. And the realization that despite having biked through the breathtaking southwestern United States and seen the sunrise through the clouds while kicking back on a glacier in the French Alps, to her mind, Antarctica is the most spectacular spot on earth.

I know what some of you are thinking: You heart penguins and Orcas and the Northern Lights as much as the next nature bunny, but that still doesn't explain why on earth Traci willingly subjected herself to subzero-temperature winters without daylight for four months (which, by the way, prompts an annual exodus of more than 80 percent of McMurdo's population). Blame it on the once-in-a-lifetime factor and her burning desire to rack up as many new experiences as possible while she's young and untethered.

I realize subscribing to the brass-ring life philosophy doesn't necessarily endear a gal to living out of a duffel bag year after year, with only her parents' basement or a storage unit to call home. And maybe your idea of work has nothing to do with moon boots, shovels, and polar ice caps and everything to do with cosmopolitan business meccas or primitive villages in the developing world. Not to worry—there's a travel gig out there for every time frame, temperament, and budget. Whether you're looking for a two-week volunteer vacation, a summertime adrenaline gig, or long-term work overseas, consider this chapter your compass. With the right amount of planning, anyone can pull a Traci Macnamara, no matter how long or short lived. So dust off your backpack, folks. It's time to hit the road.

WHY WAIT?

"Anyone who says doing the Peace Corps in Botswana or acting in a Shakespeare festival is a waste of time needs to crawl back into their office space," writes Colleen Kinder in *Delaying the Real World: A Twentysomething's Guide to Seeking Adventure.* Fun factor aside, if you're looking to make a living in the international arena, the more passport stamps and home-soil adventures you rack up, the more you'll impress potential employers.

But don't shell out hundreds or thousands in airfare just to wow some fictitious future employer—do it for yourself because you're itching to explore. In those years when you're not sure what you want to do next, where you want to live, or who you want to spend your time with (a.k.a the Pre-Mortgage Era), travel work can point you in thrilling new directions you may never have considered. That's exactly what happened to twenty-nine-year-old Jennifer Foltz. One summer during college, she took a gig on the "slime line" at an Alaskan fishery, processing fresh catches. Though the work was gross and the hours grueling, she had the time of her life and fell in love with the last frontier. As soon as she finished school in the Lower 48, she moved north, where she now works as a bush pilot.

Attorney Lisa Herb also has her travels to thank for her current work situation. While living in Mongolia for a year and a half with her wildlife biologist husband (and telecommuting to her lawyer job back in the States), she spent a good deal of her spare time volunteering for local women's rights organizations. She was so taken with the work that when she and her husband returned to the States, she started Alliance for International Women's Rights, a United States–based nonprofit organization that trains other volunteers (telecommuters and travelers alike) to help the Mongolian human rights groups she befriended. Today Lisa divides her work week between her law contracts and her nonprofit labor of love.

With every financial responsibility, relationship, and dependent you accumulate, it becomes harder to disengage from daily life and hit the road—even for a month or a season, let alone a year or two. Yes, jobs can be jettisoned, apartments or houses can be sublet, belongings can be boxed up in basements, and pets can be sent to curl up with your Aunt Judy for extended stays. Taube Gensler, a thirty-five-year-old from Phoenix, did all of the above in preparation for her move to Japan, where she's finishing her first of two years teaching English to schoolchildren. But it wasn't easy. She and her husband, a ceramic artist who tagged along for the ride, spent a number of harried months closing up their life in Arizona first.

My point is, whether it's a longer-term international career you're after or a short-lived tryst, the sooner you get on it, the better. It may help if you don't think about travel work as an all-or-nothing prospect. You don't have to permanently derail your life in the States to see the world. Instead, think of travel work as a detour. Believe me, the cube will still be waiting when you get back. But don't you wait till the end of your life to start living it. By then, your idea of adventure may be a nice cold glass of lemonade and a game of Mah-Johngg by the pool at the retirement home.

WHERE DO YOU WANT TO WORK TODAY?

As with wading into the nonprofit arena, before you dip a toe into the wonderful world of travel work, it helps to figure out what kind of adventure you're after, where you want this escapade to occur, and how long you want it to last. Are you up for manual labor, or is classroom instruction or office work more your speed? Do you crave a summer gig as a hired hand on an organic farm, an extended stay in a world-class city on the Pacific Rim, or a couple weeks helping rebuild homes in Louisiana? The friendly skies outside your airplane window are pretty much the limit.

While this section can't cover all the far-flung adventures out there, it will give you a glimpse into some of the most popular ways to blend work with travel. I didn't bother covering staples like the Peace Corps, AmeriCorps, and Habitat for Humanity, since it's my suspicion that most sentient beings have a pretty good grasp of what these programs entail. If not, a wealth of information is just a mouse-click away.

Work-permit programs. "The bad news about working abroad," reads the University of Michigan's International Center website, "is that you can't just hop a plane to any country and start looking for a job." Reason being, you need a work permit before you can work legally in another nation. And you need a job offer before you nab yourself one of those golden work permits. The good news is, if you're a student, you can get a work permit through an organization like the British Universities North America Club (BUNAC) before you arrive at your destination and commence job hunting. For a few hundred dollars, you not only cut through the red tape, you get advice (and sometimes leads) on housing and short-term jobs.

¿Habla inglés? If you're not eligible for BUNAC or not interested in job hunting on foreign soil, you can apply for an overseas gig through one of the myriad work-abroad programs out there. And unless you have a highly specialized skill, teaching English abroad, like Taube does, is your best bet. The demand is high and the openings span the globe. In fact, in Japan, where Taube teaches through a

Sister Cities program, English is a required language starting in seventh grade, meaning the opportunities to teach abound (and the pay is often nothing to sneeze at). To start your ESL job hunt, check out sites like Dave's ESL Café (ESLCafé.com) and TeachAbroad.com. In many cases, taking a Teaching English as a Second Language (TESL) course can boost your chances of getting hired.

Adrenaline gigs. "I made enough money in the summer to live off of in the winter. It's like being a crab fisherman in Alaska," says Bree Loewen, twenty-five, who worked as a climbing ranger on Mount Rainier in Washington state for three consecutive seasons. Besides having eight months off a year to knit, rock climb, and do however she pleased, the Seattle-area outdoor diva relished her eight-days-on, six-days-off work schedule on the mountain, not to mention all those opportunites to save lives and summit the peak each summer.

But climbing buffs like Bree aren't the only thrill-seekers who stand to earn while they play. River-rafting guides, ski patrols, and national park tour guides are some of the many adrenaline and outdoor gigs you'll find on sites like JobMonkey.com and AlaskaJobFinder.com. If you want to throw your fleece hat into the ring for one of these gigs, pay attention to annual or seasonal application deadlines so you don't miss your window of opportunity.

Volunteer vacations. Christy Cook is this amazing fiftysomething computer consultant/midwife I know who has been traveling solo to developing communities in Central America, South America, Asia, and Africa for the past decade, helping deliver babies and educating women as she goes. Though she prefers to arrive without an itinerary, it's only a matter of days before she finds herself amidst some thrilling project or other, like helping indigenous women start a midwifery clinic. "Connecting with women, especially around pregnancy and birth, is a way you can leapfrog over some of those cultural boundaries," she says.

Christy's usually abroad for months on end, returning to the States only to catch up with family and friends and take on some consulting work to fund her next trip. If you want to create your own mini—Peace Corps like Christy but aren't sure where to start, enroll yourself in a language school in your country of choice. Besides becoming more conversant with the locals, you'll get the inside scoop on what community projects you can help with, from building websites for local businesses to building a daycare center.

If you're not up for winging it, organizations like Alliance for International Women's Rights, Crooked Trails, and Global Citizen Journey are happy to set you up on a volunteer vacation. Many of these nonprofit groups charge a program fee of a couple thousand dollars or more per trip (airfare not included). To offset the cost, some voluntourists hold fundraisers, just as they would if running a marathon for, say, breast cancer research. As Leslye Wood, the Global Citizen Journey communications guru, explains, after educating family and friends about what your program fee will help fund—for example, human labor and construction supplies for a new library in an impoverished Nigerian village—family and friends are more likely to pony up a donation.

Contracting 202. Numerous employment agencies exist for the sole purpose of placing highly skilled healthcare professionals, like nurses, physical therapists, and radiologists, in short-term contracts around the country and globe. Wisconsin native Katie Kuijper, thirty-two, took advantage of the opportunity to spend two years sampling communities in the Southwest and Alaska—traveling for a few weeks between every contract, of course. She's since put down roots in Anchorage with her nautical-engineer husband (who also works short-term travel gigs, only out at sea).

But healthcare professionals and sailors don't hold a monopoly on exportable vocations. Through the Fulbright Teacher Exchange Program, educators can trade places with an overseas counterpart for a semester or year, and education administrators can swap spots for several weeks. And through Geekcorps, techies can spend four months volunteering to help a community in the developing world pump up its computing infrastructure.

Travel writing. Depending on who you ask, writing a guidebook for travel publishers like Moon or Lonely Planet is either the most fantastic way to subsidize your trip to a remote part of the country or world, or utterly moronic. Reason being, guidebook work simply doesn't pay much. And taking in the Turkish bathhouses while taking notes does drain some of the fun out of it. Still, for someone wanting to break into freelance writing, writing a guidebook can open up a lot of doors. It certainly did for Dorothy Waldman, author of *The Biker's Guide to Texas: 25 Great Motorcycle Rides in the Lone Star State,* who now lectures on the biker's philosophy of life and receives her fair share of related writing assignments.

Working on staff at an international publication or at an overseas bureau of a U.S. newspaper or magazine is another option. But Amanda Castleman, a thirty-one-year-old travel writer who spends three to four months on the road, says that in her book, freelancing is the only way to go. Without the leash of an editorial desk job, she's free to traipse from Hong Kong to Capetown to Honningsvåg and back

ANTI 9 to 5 tip

As you've probably gathered from the examples in this section, some travel, seasonal, and adventure gigs pay a respectable salary and benefits, while others merely offer a stipend. Still others pay nothing at all. Some come with free room and board or subsidized housing. Others expect you to rent your own place and foot your own dinner bill. But as I said earlier, travel gigs exist for every budget. It's up to you to do the detective work.

again, selling her stories to her cache of publishing contacts along the way. To learn more about travel writing, see sites like WrittenRoad.com and UGoGurl.com, check out Lonely Planet's *Travel Writing* guide, or take a class.

Green acres. Many back-to-the-land types will tell you country living feels like a permanent vacation. What's more, it's far less pricey than city dwelling. But before you sign up to work as an innkeeper's assistant, harvest veggies on an organic farm, or crush vineyard grapes, know what you're getting into—especially if you're an urban cowgirl. Romantic notions don't always match up to reality. Some people panic once wildlife, septic tanks, and freaky weather patterns come into play. Ditto for how very, very dark the path to your sleeping quarters can be.

If you do have a genuine interest in the simple life (sans Paris and Nicole) check out organizations like Worldwide Opportunities on Organic Farms (www.wwoof.org). Also see the camp, ranch, and resort gigs listed on BackDoorJobs.com and CoolWorks.com.

SCORING AN INTERNATIONAL GIG

Maybe slinging salmon in Alaska last summer or your recent volunteer vacation in Venezuela did little to curb your appetite for adventure. And maybe in your staff-meeting daydreams back in the Lower 48, you see a sunny new life for yourself working and living in Egypt. Or Ecuador. Or Estonia. For the next three to five years. So how do you make yourself more attractive to those in the hiring seats?

As you would when embarking on any career path, you have to start collecting experiences—both paid and unpaid international work, at your present job or otherwise. If you currently work for a company with offices overseas, volunteer to take part in international projects, even if they're not part of your job description. Then get to know your overseas counterparts and network like mad. If it's a transfer you covet, the same rules for winning over the higher-ups discussed earlier in the book apply: Pay your dues, prove you're invaluable, and make a solid case for why relocating you to China would benefit the company. "I've always wanted to see the Great Wall" is not a valid business case. "We need an on-site liaison with the Asian business development team, and I'm just the (impeccably qualified) woman to do it" is.

If there's no international arm at your company, don't despair. There's lots more you can do to boost your Good On Paper quotient. If you already travel on your own, good. Keep at it. Backpack. Volunteer in developing villages. Hone your knowledge of world affairs. "Employers want to make sure someone's going to be able to handle the challenges of living abroad, dealing with other families, and speaking other languages—being able to live in another culture, basically," says Chicago resident Gia Pionek, thirty-five, who's lived and worked on five continents. "Just having traveled other places makes you more attractive, because it at least shows you can handle changing money and all the other little annoyances."

Picking up a second language is also key. "Learning the language is more than just memorizing the words," says Lynn Shiori Miyauchi, who works at the Consulate-General of Japan in Seattle. Employers want to see that you grasp cultural nuances and can follow the cues of others. Studying at a language school, as mentioned earlier, is a fantastic way to go. After conjugating verbs in another language all day, it's natural to want to run out at night and put your newfound vocabulary to the test. And what better way to get your daily dose of cultural immersion?

Another way to score Brownie points is by volunteering with other cultures right here in the States—a great option for those on a tight budget or with scant vacation time. Taube taught ESL to kids in her Phoenix community because she knew she wanted to teach abroad. It was a good primer for her, and a nice addition to her resume. Extra credit that the work directly related to the overseas teaching program she applied for.

Whether you're volunteering, studying, or doing your first paid contract abroad, make the most of your time there. "Don't just party," Miyauchi says. Bring those business cards and network just as you would in the States. In fact, plane rides are among the best places to network, since you'll find more English speakers on them.

THE SAVVY TRAVELER

To ensure your working vacation goes as smoothly and safely as possible, veteran jet-setters recommend you start planning months in advance. Once you've settled on a destination and work program, give yourself a crash course in the social customs, transportation system, and exchange rate there (speed-reading a guidebook on the plane won't cut it). Besides ingesting your fill of off-the-beaten-path travel books, read the country's fiction and poetry. "That's how you get a real glimpse into a culture," says Holly Morris, author of *Adventure Divas: Searching the Globe for a New Kind of Heroine.*

Next, brush up on any key phrases in Spanish, Slovak, or Swahili you think you'll need. "Always know at least twenty words of vocabulary and try, try, try to speak it," Morris says. "Don't worry about butchering the language. People appreciate the effort, and being made fun of—which will inevitably happen [to you]—is a terrific bonding experience."

But don't just rely on your bookshelf to school you. Use Yahoo! Groups and web forums like ThornTree.LonelyPlanet.com and VirtualTourist.com to talk with other adventure-chasers who've traveled, studied, or worked where you're headed. Talk to people in person, too. Email and online forums don't give you the whole story, cautions Taube, the ESL teacher in Japan. Also be sure to ask about the conditions of your destination. Before you buy that plane ticket, be honest with yourself: Can you really hang with the no-bathroom situation? If not, go elsewhere. There's no shame in embracing one's preference for modern plumbing.

Now for the logistics: You'll need to ensure your passport's up to date, secure the necessary visas, and get the appropriate shots before you go. You'll also need travel insurance. "Considering that the average cost of a medical evacuation overseas is over $50,000, comprehensive medical insurance that covers evacuation is critical," Colleen Kinder writes in *Delaying the Real World*. Enough said. (Helpful websites for all this stuff are in the "Must-See Resources" section of the appendix.)

ANTI 9 to 5 tip

Give some thought to what you'll wear on your overseas adventure—in some locales, your well-being depends on it. Elaine Lee author of *Go Girl! The Black Woman's Book of Travel & Adventure*, recommends leaving any fancy jewelry or spendy clothes at home and instead dressing modestly, "unless you are in Paris, of course." And as retro as it may seem, abiding by any local dress codes for women, like donning the veil in Iran, is a must. "[Shunning] dress codes is not the most effective way to assert your political beliefs," Morris says. "In some countries, 'dressing right' means staying out of prison."

Don't leave home without it

Once you've squared away your passport, plowed through a couple guide-books, and memorized critical phrases such as *"¿Dónde está el baño?"* you can focus on what really matters: packing. If you plan to live out of a back-pack for a few weeks or months, what you bring and how you bring it can greatly impact your sunny disposition.

The first rule of thumb is, of course, to only pack what you can carry. I know it sounds obvious, but if I had a buck for every time a supposedly travel-savvy girlfriend showed up for a camping trip with more than she could hoist on her back (and then expected me to pick up the slack), well, you get the idea. . . . Don't be the woman with the bag she can't lift—you'll never get over the shame, and you'll alienate people before even opening your mouth.

To combat the temptation to overpack, veteran travelers recommend laying out every item you want to bring and then halving the pile. "Do you really want to tote around an umbrella, or fourteen T-shirts, or six sizes of Band-Aids?" says *Adventure Divas* author Holly Morris. "In most countries you can buy everything that you might unexpectedly need (or make do)."

Besides remembering your passport and mad money, packing your own little MacGyver Kit can make your trip breezier and, in some cases, help you win friends and influence people, no matter where you land. Herewith, a checklist from some of the most seasoned jet-setters I know. Feel free to mix and match, depending on where you're going, how long you're traveling for, and how you're traveling.

❑ *Copies of key documents.* When on the go, always keep copies of your passport, visa, work permit, credit card, phone card, and any other essentials—at home and in your travel bag, Morris says.

❑ *Duct tape.* "You will find 10,000 uses for it, like leaving notes, tap-ing up sarongs (another Never Leave Home Without) on curtainless windows, fixing rips, et cetera," says my friend Karen, a Philadelphia grammar school teacher who spends her summers backpacking in exotic climes.

❏ *Emergency undies.* Pack a fresh pair in your carry-on, along with any essential toiletries and a change or two of clothes. If your luggage gets lost (as it invariably will), you're good to go. Speaking of toiletries, stash some tampons in your backpack. Gyno items (condoms too) can be tough to track down or pricey to score on the road, Morris warns.

❏ *Plastic bags.* Lining your backpack with garbage bags can be a lifesaver during downpours. "And when fire ants invade your personal belongings, you can pull everything out in one fell swoop (as opposed to pulling clothes out piece by piece and incurring the wrath of the ants)," Karen says.

❏ *T-shirts to trade.* What better way to memorialize friendships forged on the road? Besides, Morris says, "Wouldn't you rather have an East Zermatt Yodeling Camp 1989 T-shirt than some boring old New York Yankees T-shirt?" My friend Valerie, a Seattle schoolteacher and summer traveler, takes this one step further, bringing postcards from home to bestow upon locals, as well as new friends she wants to give her U.S. contact information to.

❏ *A piece of rope.* "It's like the *Hitchhiker's Guide* towel," Valerie says. Use your trusty rope as a clothesline, a way to secure your bag to your bed if traveling by train, and a way to tie two twin beds together for romantic interludes (proof-tested by Valerie and her beau in Holland).

❏ *Bug spray.* Karen recommends the roll-on DEET kind to avoid having the wind blow any spray into your face or chew small holes through your glasses (which, she learned the hard way, it will).

❏ *Wet wipes.* A great way to stay clean(ish), even when there's no shower in sight. Comes in handy if you need to wash up before dinner, too. Rinse 'n Go can also can keep you fresh in more rural locales when you're down to your last duds. After all, nothing beats a clean pair of socks.

❏ *A talisman.* Call her superstitious, but Morris never leaves home without her Sky Dancer doll. Besides the rabbit's-foot factor, it gives you a slice of home when you're thousands of miles away.

Don't be afraid to travel solo. "You're never alone longer than twenty-four hours," says Elaine Lee, author of *Go Girl!* You're bound to meet fellow travelers and locals, many of whom will invite you to dine with them. Bring names and numbers of friends of friends living where you're headed, so you have a welcoming soul to break bread with when you land, as well as an emergency contact should things go awry. And be careful not to hide in an expat bubble—it's the quickest route to feeling like a tourist.

As far as safety, the U.S. Department of State website (www.travel .state.gov) posts travel advisories for any don't-go-there-if-you-know-what's-good-for-you regions. If you find yourself suddenly drowning in a sea of civil unrest, as my friend June did while visiting Lebanon during the summer of 2006, take your cues from the local moms. "When they start packing, you do too," Morris says. Besides steering clear of war-torn nations, listen to your gut and avoid shady characters, just as you would at home.

Finally, be willing to wing it. When cultures collide, it's inevitable things won't always go according to plan. The best travelers are those who can channel their inner flower child and go with the flow.

SHOW ME THE MONEY

Obviously, you'll want to book your flight well ahead of time to snag the best airfare you can. I'm a fan of travel sites like Orbitz and Expedia; you may have other favorites. Just be sure to read the fine print. If you're a frequent flyer, get a credit card that gives you miles when you buy, and do your best to stick with one airline so you amass a decent amount of miles before the next century.

Avoid waiting till the last minute to renew your passport and obtain visas so you don't rack up rush fees. Depending on where you're headed, a passport that's due to expire in six months or less won't do you an ounce of good. Check the U.S. Department of State website (www.state.gov) for details, fees, and deadlines.

If you're planning a volunteer vacation by your lonesome (rather than through a travel program) or looking for a place to land before your travel gig starts, you can save a bundle by staying off the beaten path. Besides steering clear of tourist traps and hotels (not to mention traveling during the off-season), rooming with friends of friends of friends or at youth hostels can save you a pretty penny. For some of the best deals on global lodging, *Delaying the Real World* author Colleen Kinder recommends splurging for a $28 membership to Hostelling International—USA (www.hiusa.org), which she calls "AAA for young backpackers." To break bread with the locals *and* save your dollars, check out homestay organizations like Servas.org (nominal fee and interview required), GlobalFreeloaders.com, HospitalityClub .org, and CouchSurfing.com.

Saving for a global gig's travel or relocation costs is much like saving for any vacation. If my handful of single, underpaid U.S. schoolteacher pals (half of whom have mortgages) can spend their summers globe-trotting, surely you can figure out a way to finance your plane ticket to that ESL gig in Egypt. My friend Valerie's travel-fundraising poison of choice is to get a retail job over the holidays, but maybe you'd rather hold a virtual yard sale on eBay, take a high-paying contract gig for a few months, or give up coffee and beer for a stretch.

Those who routinely work in national parks or impoverished villages find living frugally (and, consequently, socking away the cash) a no-brainer. "When I'm in the States, I try really hard to live simply," says Christy Cook, the volunteer midwife. "I think my living in poor countries has taught me how to do that. Now every time I walk into a grocery store and I see eighteen different brands of toilet paper, I think, *Why the hell do we need all these?*"

No matter how you raise or save the cash, stow it in a separate bank account so you're not tempted to dip into it. Otherwise, it's too easy to pretend you'll start saving next month. More often than not, you wind up putting the whole trip on your credit card, which you'll live to regret once you get back home. Whatever you do, don't ask your parents for a handout, unless it's for a good cause, like a volunteer vacation with a group like Global Citizen Journey. If they're already less than keen on your itinerary (some parents get antsy just thinking about the term "developing country") and you wind up in some Third World hospital with a nasty case of dysentery, as happened to a friend of mine, you'll have to hear about it for the rest of your days, which likely will trump the dysentery itself in the pain-and-suffering department.

ANTI 9-TO-5 ACTION PLAN

ESL teacher Taube Gensler pretty much said it all when she told me, "The kids I teach asked me, 'What is your dream?' And I said, 'I'm living my dream. I'm in Japan.'" When it comes to work options for would-be jet-setters, this chapter is just the tip of the iceberg. In other words, time to get research happy. Books and websites brimming with ideas abound. You'll find a few I like best in the "Must-See Resources" section of the appendix.

As always, customize the information in this action plan to fit your own situation and dream gig, be it a two-week excursion or a two-year stint as an expat.

STAGE 1: KNOW WHERE YOU'LL GO	
Start date	Checklist
	Decide what kind of place, culture, and gig appeal to you. Are you looking for an outdoor adventure, one in a cosmopolitan region, or one in the developing world?
	Figure out how much dough you can afford to spend, how long you'll transplant yourself for, and if and when you'll quit your current job.
	Determine how you'll save or raise any necessary funds you need for your trip, be it taking a second job, working extra shifts, or cutting back on coffee and new clothes.

STAGE 2: TRICK OUT YOUR TRAVELER'S RESUME	
Start date	Checklist
	Read the online bios of international and adventure workers you admire, from peers to bigwigs. Where have they gone, and what global skills have they collected along the way?
	Take a couple people who've done the type of travel work you want to do—be it volunteer, urban, rural, seasonal, or long term—to coffee for a brain-picking session.
	Extra credit: Volunteer in the States doing something related to the overseas work you covet.
	Extra credit: Lend a hand on an international project at your current job.

STAGE 3: SCOPE OUT YOUR DESTINATION	
Start date	**Checklist**
	The best part! Read the guidebooks and literature of the country or U.S. region you'd like to explore. Note details about public transportation, money, and the mother tongue.
	Narrow the travel programs you're interested in down to a shortlist, and talk to coordinators and past participants. Make sure you get a clear picture of the living conditions and job details.
	Gather up your program applications—as far in advance as you can—and submit away.

STAGE 4: COUNTDOWN TIME!	
Start date	**Checklist**
	Take care of your international paperwork: passport, visas, work permit, you name it.
	Buy your plane tix and traveler's insurance, make any necessary lodging accommodations, and consider getting an international driver's license.
	Pack up your worldly possessions for the storage unit, sublet your pad, and send pets to their interim home.
	Ask friends (and friends of friends) for names and numbers of locals who live where you're headed.
	Extra credit: Study the native language a few months ahead of time, or arrange to take classes while abroad.

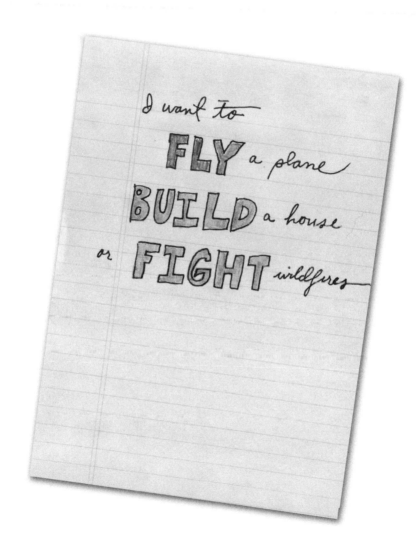

chapter 9

I want to
FLY a plane
BUILD a house
or FIGHT wildfires

"I know something of a woman in a man's profession.

Yes, by God, I do know about that."

—Dame Judi Dench as Queen Elizabeth in *Shakespeare in Love,* 1998

Angela Cimato's parents wanted her to be a secretary. Sicilian immigrants who moved to New York in 1963, they believed a woman's place in the world had more to do with serving men than with following a path of her choosing. It was just their cultural mindset. So you can imagine how they reacted to the news that Angela wanted to attend Embry-Riddle Aeronautical University in Florida to study space physics in hopes of one day becoming a NASA astronaut. "Hit the roof" would be one way to describe it.

Hardly one to be deterred (after graduating high school, Angela moved to England for a year to be a nanny, despite her parents' protests), she smiled and nodded politely through her parents' lectures about how foolish she was being. She wasn't about to let her parents' Old World ideas about suitable career choices for women stand in her way.

When someone says, "I love that we can build a machine to send people out of Earth's orbit, into the orbit of another celestial being. I love that we can put a robot on another planet. I love the idea of someday being the first person to set foot on Mars," you know she's been dreaming of a career in space for a long time. In fact, Angela first had her mind blown by physics in a required science class in high school. And so, despite the lack of support from her family, she applied to the school she coveted (attending a New York college for a year when she didn't get in the first time) and secured the loans and part-time work she needed to pay her tuition, room, and board.

I talked to the twenty-four-year-old during her junior year at Embry-Riddle, a school with a student body that's 85 percent male. When she wasn't busy studying or taking practice flights, she was volunteering for NASA or teaching high school girls about job opportunities in science and the space industry. Every step of the way she's held to a much higher standard than her male peers, and every step of the way she gives it everything she's got—from her grades to the classes she teaches to her volunteer projects. To Angela, who emailed me one night ecstatic that she got to sleep under the Saturn V moon rocket at Cape Canaveral, the payoff is more than worth it. "Imagine women of my grandmother's generation studying to be an astronaut—it was impossible," she says. "Imagine what our grandchildren are going to accomplish after us. . . ."

Yes, we've come a long way, baby. But considering the wage gap and paltry percentages of women in this country's stereotypically "male" fields, it's clear we still have light-years to go. If you want to fly a plane or build a skyscraper or fight fires, don't let the statistics stop you. In this chapter, you'll get tips on navigating ultra-male-dominated fields from engineers, pilots, women in uniform, women in the trades, and a woman of the cloth. The same researching and networking tactics covered throughout the book apply here, too. And as you'll see in these pages, there are plenty of professional groups that women in traditionally male fields can turn to for career advice and support.

Although most of these gigs involve working for an employer, none of them are snoozy desk jobs. Many have flexible or shift-based schedules that are anything but 9 to 5. Others involve physical labor and working outside at least part of the time. Even if you're not looking for anything quite as daring as space travel or emergency rescue work, I suspect you'll find the suggestions in this chapter relevant to any job where you're the odd woman out—be it filmmaking, farming, forensics, or financial management. So prepare for liftoff, people. It's time to boldly go where most women (and many men) have not gone before.

ME AND THE BOYS

A s women like Angela will tell you, working in aviation, fire-fighting, or construction—where just a fraction of your colleagues are likely to be female—has its unique set of challenges. Even in this day and age, comments and attitudes of the "What's a nice little girl like you doing in a man's job?" nature do arise.

Lily Iftner, thirty-two, who runs her own civil engineering consulting business in Seattle, heard, "Are you the secretary?" a lot during her first year working on construction sites (despite being clad in a hardhat and work boots). And Angela, the astronaut-in-training, had her share of competitive male classmates snub her if she tried to share news of a particularly exciting flight she'd piloted. On the other hand, if she had a bad flight, those same classmates would relish every humiliating detail. "Suddenly, I was the worst pilot in the universe because I made some rookie mistake that they too have made several times," she says.

But sometimes cluelessness and hazing are more products of the macho job culture than anything else. "I think I actually got more ribbing for being Canadian than for being a woman," says geotechnical engineer Carolyn Anderson, who spends 25 percent of her work week on construction sites. And at Alaskan bush pilot Jennifer Foltz's first gig, the senior pilots dubbed the newbies—guys and gals alike—FNG, short for Fucking New Guy. Translation: "You don't know shit and you can't fly, rookie."

The quickest road to respect in a male-dominated field, these groundbreaking gals say, is to work your tail off. "In my classes, I have to be pretty damned sure that what I say isn't going to make me (and all women) look stupid before I raise my hand," Angela says. Maintaining your professionalism at all times is key, too. That includes dressing for a construction site, not date night. "You just can't walk into an office of all men wearing a spaghetti-strap tank top," says Traci Macnamara, who spent six months working alongside thirteen male mechanics at McMurdo Station in Antarctica. "That's not professional, unless maybe you're a swimsuit model." Tami St. Paul, training coordinator of an International Union of Operating Engineers apprenticeship program, has this to say: "People will treat you how you approach them. If you approach them with a flirty little looking-for-a-husband attitude, that's how you'll be treated."

Asking thoughtful questions on the job is a must. Number one, you'll figure out what the heck is going on. Number two, when the seasoned guys you work with see you're serious about learning the ropes, "they'll eat it up," St. Paul says. From what she's seen in her twenty years in construction, the guys take great pride in their work and are happy to share what they know with a willing student. "If your attitude is great, I don't think it matters what [gender] you are," she says. Carolyn, the geotechnical engineer, notes that women may have the advantage here. She's seen many a male rookie wrestle with his ego when it comes to asking for directions on a construction site.

ANTI 9-to-5 tip

Having male mentors is all well and good, but you also need support where the boys aren't. "Men can give great advice, but when it comes down to it, they just don't get being a woman and being in ministry. How could they?" says Mary Beth Mardis-LeCroy, a twenty-eight-year-old minister at a Presbyterian church in Des Moines, Iowa. Cozy up to other women who do what you do—at your workplace and otherwise. You'll need their support. That's what organizations like Women in the Fire Service and National Association of Women in Construction are there for.

More often than not, these women say, once you prove yourself to be the capable, kick-ass woman you are, the guys not only respect you, they look out for you like a brother would, and one-big-happy-family mode ensues. Sure, it's not fair that we have to work twice as hard to get ahead, but until more guys get with the program and more women enter these fields, it's part of the territory. Besides, as Angela puts it, those double standards make us women "appreciate our successes that much more."

THE OTHER NAYSAYERS

Sometimes it's not the male colleagues who make the thoughtless comments or ask the inane questions. Civilians occasionally come up to San Francisco firefighter Karen Kerr, thirty-seven, and ask if she and her female coworkers do the same job as the men. Not only do the women carry the same eighty to 100 pounds of axes, chain saws, ladders, hoses, and extinguishers as the men, they get paid the same salary.

For Bree Loewen, who worked on Mount Rainier for three years, it was the people attempting to summit the mountain who had trouble grasping the concept of a female ranger, not to mention one who could save their ass as well as a man. Many male climbers who approached the ranger station with questions about weather and route conditions refused to look at her directly. Instead, they would address question after question to her non-ranger boyfriend (who often visited her at the station), despite the fact that Bree was the one with the ranger uniform on. "I would answer the question, and they would continue to look at Russell and talk to him. It was like this weird triangle. That happened so many times," she says.

And for Pastor Mardis-LeCroy, it's the Southern Baptist side of her family that's having a bit of trouble divining that she's breaking the stained-glass ceiling. "What I do as a woman is so totally out of their vocabulary," she says. "It's as if I'm going up to them and saying,

---

Women who paved the way

Career firsts for women hardly begin and end with pre–World War II pioneers like Amelia Earhart, who in 1932 became the first woman to fly solo across the Atlantic. Check out these recent firsts:

✐ NASA astronaut Eileen Collins became the first woman to pilot an American space shuttle (Discovery) in 1995 and the first woman to command an American space shuttle (Columbia) in 1999.

✐ Madeleine Albright became the first female secretary of state in 1997, which, at the time, made her the highest-ranking woman in the history of U.S. government.

✐ Judith Brewer became the world's first female career firefighter (as opposed to volunteer) in 1974. She was hired by the Arlington County, Virginia, fire department.

✐ Barbara Walters became the first female nightly news anchor on network television in 1976.

✐ Susan Roley and Joanne Pierce, the first women to become FBI agents, completed their training in 1972.

✐ Ensign Jean Marie Butler graduated from the Coast Guard Academy in 1980, making her the first woman to graduate from a U.S. service academy.

✐ Nancy Pelosi was elected democratic leader of the House of Representatives in 2002, making her the first woman to lead a major party in the U.S. Congress.

'Hi, it's great to see you! Have you heard what I've been up to these days? I'm an *mmnnnph.*'"

Though many of the women working in predominantly male fields that I talked to encountered sexism from time to time, none of them let it stand in their way. As Pastor Mardis-LeCroy says, learning a new language takes time—both for those still trying to adjust to the changing social landscape and for those pioneering the changes.

HARASSMENT REVISITED:
KNOW WHAT YOU'LL DO

"When I first came on the job twenty-three years ago, fighting fires was the easiest part of the job for me. Much harder was dealing with the hatred and discrimination that some male firefighters had for me," Captain Brenda Berkman says in an interview on the PBS webpage for the documentary "Taking the Heat: The First Women Firefighters of New York City."

If you think big bad discrimination battles like Berkman's went the way of the dodo when feminists started burning their bras, think again. Gender bias in the workplace is alive and well, as the 23,094 charges of sex-based discrimination made to the U.S. Equal Employment Opportunity Commission in the 2005 fiscal year will attest. In fact, as I write this in June 2006, the U.S. Supreme Court just made a high-profile ruling in favor of a forklift operator whose supervisors had given her grief for working while female and then penalized her (with demotions, suspensions, and the like) for complaining about the unfair treatment.

But enough about worse-case scenarios. Let's talk about the aspects of the job you *can* control. The real trick to thriving in a traditionally male field is knowing what you'll do if a higher-up swats your ass (been there), a coworker tells you in graphic detail what he'd like to do to the "hot new lady boss" (there too), or your suggestions are met with blank stares at staff meetings (yep). "Know when you'll say when," says Traci, the seasoned Antarctica laborer. "Have boundaries going into it." The last thing you want to do is freak out on the spot. A healthy dose of forethought can help you keep your cool. So before you start the gig, rehearse what you'll say and whom you'll say it to should sexism rear its ugly head. Will you tell the offending party to stop? Will you walk away and later confide in a female coworker or friend? Will you tell your boss? Your boss's boss? A professional association you belong to?

A sense of humor is essential, as many women I talked to will attest. "Being able to laugh at testosterone-fueled jokes is more therapeutic than getting offended by them," says Angela, the astronaut-in-training. That said, don't be afraid to speak up and stand your ground—it's the only way anything's ever going to change. Angela's certainly not one to back down: Once, while taking flight lessons at school, a guy in her program was sitting in on her flight as an observer. Before takeoff, the guy got snarky with Angela and said, "You shouldn't be a pilot. You should be a flight attendant." Unfortunately for him, Angela had planned to practice taking steep turns during the flight, high-angle maneuvers that would make "any unaccustomed stomach nauseous." As you can probably guess, Angela was happy to report, "His was an unaccustomed stomach. Karma's a fierce warrior!"

ANTI 9 to 5 tip

Always know what you're getting into, advises Cindia Cameron, organizing director of 9to5, the National Association of Working Women. Before you start any gig, try to get the inside scoop from other women in the field. Read up on the workplace culture and look at the company manuals. Is there a section on harassment and discrimination that tells you how to lodge a complaint? (If not, take heed.) Also, acquaint yourself with sexual-discrimination law (federal and state) so you know exactly what behaviors are legally verboten.

GETTING OVER THE BLUE-COLLAR STIGMA

If your parents and high school guidance counselors are anything like mine were, college was the Holy Grail, and nothing short of a four-year university degree would do. Working in
the trades—physically demanding work like carpentry, landscaping, electrical work, plumbing, and firefighting—was what kids who
excelled in wood shop did after graduation. Respectable young
women worked in offices, not overalls! Respectable young women
didn't work on a construction site, they crafted letters! Presentations! Quarterly reports!

I hope you know this couldn't be further from the truth. "So many
people who come through our school are disillusioned by office
jobs," says Beth Arman, dean of trade and industry apprenticeship at
Renton Technical College in Washington state. What's more, many
of her school's students, who have an average age of thirty-three, *have*
gone to college and are now looking for either a career change or a
more marketable job skill.

Firefighter Karen Kerr fits this profile to a T. Karen, who has a
master's in women's studies and is an avid outdoorswoman, spent
three years working indoors in healthcare research before firefighting ignited her interest, and she tore through the competitive, rig-
orous process of applying, training, and testing for the job. "Most
people feel really lucky that they do this for a living," she says. "It's no
office job." Instead, it's hands on, heart pumping, physically grueling, and the most fun she's ever had making a living.

In *Generation Debt: Why Now Is a Terrible Time to Be Young,* author Anya
Kamenetz argues for debunking the stigma surrounding vocational
and technical education, especially at the high school level. Doing so
could conceivably save twentysomethings a lot of time and money,
considering more than half of all college students are too broke,
exhausted from juggling day jobs, or disillusioned to finish their
degree. Besides, as Kamenetz points out, "no more than one-third
of jobs in this economy require a four-year degree or more."

The beauty of unions

Union women fare better than their nonunion counterparts. Check out these statistics from the friendly folks at 9to5, National Association of Working Women, and the national coalition Tradeswomen Now and Tomorrow.

- In 2004, 43 percent of all union workers were women.
- The typical female union member earns 34 percent more than a woman who doesn't belong to a union.
- Women of color who belong to a union earn almost 35 percent more than nonunion women of color.
- Women represented by unions earn almost 87 percent as much as union men (as opposed to the 77 percent of the male dollar their nonunion counterparts earn).
- Over a thirty-year career, a journey-level (i.e., upper-echelon) electrician will make over $1 million more than a childcare worker. Ouch.

It's also high time we took away the blue-collar stigma regarding *women*, given that the salaries and benefits of trade gigs blow those of lower-rung office, service, or retail gigs out of the water. Sure, physical labor isn't for everyone, as evidenced by the fact that fewer than 3 percent of all construction workers are women. But for women who relish the idea, it can be extremely lucrative.

According to Nontraditional Employment for Women, an organization that has trained many of New York City's female hardhats, the average salary for a home healthcare aide in New York is $18,000, while it's $53,000 for a construction worker. In Seattle, many trade apprenticeships start at $14 to $20 an hour, and wages around $30 or more an hour are common for veterans (a.k.a. journeymen). Throw in paid apprenticeships and having a union to negotiate compensation packages for you, and you've got a pretty sweet deal.

SHOW ME THE MONEY

Though trade gigs require a lot of training—physical, mechanical, and classroom—the good news is that you get to earn while you learn. "It's literally like a full-ride scholarship," says Tami St. Paul, the construction-apprenticeship training coordinator you met earlier. "Instead of spending eight hours a day in class, you're spending eight hours out in the field—while getting paid."

To learn more about apprenticeships in your area, check your state government website or your tradeswoman organization of choice. Know that if you're unemployed, you may be eligible for a worker-retraining program (subsidized!) at your local community college. And if you're low income, you may qualify for free pre-apprenticeship training programs in your community.

Training to be a pilot is a different story. Unlike trade work, there are no paid apprenticeships for aspiring pilots. However, there are grants and scholarships, as astronaut-to-be Angela Cimato (who covers 20 percent of her college tuition with government grants and academic scholarships) and bush pilot Jennifer Foltz (who received $15,000 in grants from the state of Alaska) will attest. For a list of scholarships, check with organizations like The Ninety-Nines (International Organization of Women Pilots) and Whirly-Girls (International Women Helicopter Pilots). You also can walk into most aviation schools and pilot your first flight (assisted, of course) for less than $100. Now that's my kind of informational interview.

ANTI 9-TO-5 ACTION PLAN

By now you should know the drill: Jane spies interesting new career path. Jane does the necessary detective work. Jane tricks out her resume and body of skills. Jane then takes a deep breath and—disregarding all naysayers—throws her hat into the ring. If you need a refresher, these steps will walk you through.

STAGE 1: SNIFF OUT THE GIG	
Start date	Checklist
	Read up on the field and its heroes—past and present. Talk to as many women and men in the field as you can.
	Visit job sites, do police or firefighter ride-alongs, or test-drive flight school to see what you think.
	Look up apprenticeship or job listings and requirements. Note application deadlines.

STAGE 2: GEAR UP TO APPLY	
Start date	Checklist
	If you're out of shape, work on that. Get acquainted with any tools (yes, those found in the garage) the job will entail.
	Take classes to fill in any blanks: Learn CPR, get your EMT license through a community college, or brush up on your knowledge of building construction.
	Send in those applications!

STAGE 3: ENSURE YOU'LL FIT IN	
Start date	Checklist
	Before you accept, scope out the workplace culture and attitudes toward women.
	Prethink how you'll react to harassment: What will you say? Who will you tell?

STAGE 4: SET YOURSELF UP FOR SUCCESS	
Start date	Checklist
	Ask for what you're worth: Research the going rate and negotiate without fear (see "No-Fear Negotiation" in the appendix for suggestions).
	Join the new girls' club: Befriend other women on the job and get involved with professional organizations.

epilogue

go forth &

CONQUER

hile I was working on this book, the women I talked to treated me to a smorgasbord of take-this-job-and-shove-it tales. One of my favorites came from a twentysomething I'll call Nina. A few years back, Nina worked as a receptionist for a boss she describes as "this tiny little man, maybe about 5' 3", who had the biggest Napoleon complex I've ever had the displeasure to witness." Getting berated by the boss in front of coworkers for things that weren't their fault was all part of the routine for Nina and the other receptionist at the company.

But one day the Little Cheese pushed Nina too far. He handed her some admin form, a poor-quality fax that was almost illegible, to fill out on the typewriter, and ordered her to make it look "as good as one of those papers you hand in to your fancy college professors." Nina did her best to make shit into Shinola, and on cue, the boss did his best to chew her out for a job badly done—for a full five minutes, in front of the entire staff. Then he called her into his office, closed the door, and told her he had the original form saved in a Word doc and would just email it to her so she could try again.

Fuming, she told him where he could stick his form, quit on the spot, and stormed out à la Dolly Parton in *Nine to Five*. But not before she took the fax machine and stuck it on top of a filing cabinet. While cleaning out her desk, she had the delectable pleasure of watching the boss "jump and struggle to see the fax machine before he had to call for the other receptionist to come get it for him—ah, pink-collar revenge."

While most of us may never experience anything quite so cinematic in our illustrious cube-monkey careers, we've all had those Dilbert moments when we realize something's got to give. If you find yourself slapping your forehead repeatedly as the CEO delivers yet another unintelligible, acronym-riddled speech, it's probably time you gave your day job a much-needed face-lift. Hopefully, the stories you've heard here from other women with alterna-careers have inspired you to poke around the Internet, peruse the bookstore shelves, sign up for a class or two, and pick the brains of those whose careers you covet.

The important thing is that you don't put off for tomorrow what's making you piss and moan today. Use the action plans in this book to help you set goals. Without them, it's far too easy to let the months whiz by without making a dent in your quest for pain-free employment. Take baby steps—fifteen minutes a day, one evening a week, whatever you can do. That way, the road before you won't seem so overwhelming. Track your progress in a notebook, spreadsheet, or with any other tool your resourceful little heart desires so you can see the fruits of your labor. And by all means, if you happen upon a golden opportunity—say, to meet with one of your career heroines or send your resume or portfolio to a company on your Top Ten list—don't blow it off. Act swiftly, and always extend the same courtesy you'd extend to your grandmother.

And don't even try to tell me you're too old, busy, or broke, or you've put in too much time arriving at the miserable career pinnacle you now find yourself at. If you're twenty-five, thirty, thirty-five, or better, you still have at least two or three decades of work ahead of you. So why not cut your losses and cut your teeth on a new vocation you may actually enjoy? The least you can do is research what else is out there. The exploration alone might energize you enough to carry you through the ho-hum 9-to-5 work week.

It may help to remind yourself that, like Madonna, many women you met in this book have undergone at least one reinvention tour. There was techie Andrea Beyer, who enrolled in cosmetology school to become a hairstylist. There was Traci Macnamara, the English professor turned Antarctica laborer. And Lisa Fitzhugh, who went from a high-powered political career to founding a nonprofit arts-education organization.

195

It may also help to remind yourself that picking one gig doesn't preclude your doing all others, so don't let option paralysis stand in your way. You met several Renaissance women with dual careers in this book, from literary agent/stand-up comic Janet Rosen, to dominatrix/freelance writer Mistress Blue, to engineer/ghost-tour guide Amy Lynwander, to real estate agent/small-business owner Krystal Perkins.

You also met several women taking the mercenary approach to earning a paycheck and doing the work they really love on the side, from attorney Lisa Herb, who also runs a nonprofit organization that benefits Mongolian women, to tech editor Lynn Finnel, who spends her summer weekends volunteering as a mountain ranger. Yes, getting a new career or solo venture off the ground while holding down a day job means more work and less free time, but I've yet to meet an entrepreneur who regrets putting in the hours. Labors of love are funny that way; when you get a rush from your work, you're happy to go the distance. As Gloria Steinem said, "I think the best job is often one that doesn't exist until you create it. The best career is one that you carve out for yourself."

That's not to say you should up and quit tomorrow without getting your ducks in a row. You'll need those contacts and letters of recommendation, fresh-off-the-grill skills, an updated resume or portfolio, and some bread-and-butter income lined up (be it a less-demanding day gig, a flex gig, or your first foray into self-employment).

As you go about the business of building up your web-design empire on the side, working an extra job to finance your Ugandan volunteer vacation, or training to be a bush pilot, there will be naysayers. Lots of them. But know this: Many of them hate their office-bot jobs (or the gigs they spent several decades toiling at before retiring) and secretly wish they had the guts you do to get out of Dodge Incorporated. Befriending those with similar aspirations can help immensely, not just with brainstorming and the swapping of war stories, but with any newfound frugality. As Kate Greenen, the financial-planning administrator who's hightailing it for a career in family counseling, says, when saving one's pennies, it's not easy hanging out with the high-rent, pricey-restaurant crowd, people seemingly better at playing The Adult Game than you.

For the record, I am not anti-corporation or anti–day job. (After all, who do you think my clients are?) Without them, many creative types would be begging for change outside their local organic grocery store. Curiously, during the final few weeks of working on these chapters, I heard from several women you met throughout the book who were suffering from what I like to think of as The Grass Is Always Greener Syndrome: Beena, the "I'll do whatever it takes to be a writer" legal assistant turned temp, was once again entertaining the notion of law school. The lack of job security was getting her down. Traci, the globe-trotter, was longing to unpack her duffel bag and fantasizing about putting down roots in Colorado, her last known permanent address. And one part-time desk jockey, whom I'll call Evangeline lest her boss reads this, went back to a full-time work schedule because she needed the dinero.

With money being such a strong motivator, we self-styled career gals would be lying if we said we didn't occasionally think of throwing in the towel and getting a more stable 9-to-5 job. If you give the anti 9-to-5 life a test run and decide it isn't for you, or if you love it but the Desk Job of the Century comes along, there's no shame in taking it. Even some of the most indie-minded solo artists get pulled back into Jobville when they least expect it, just like Don Michael Corleone in *The Godfather: Part III*. And while I've never whacked anyone, I'm no stranger to this flip-flopping. A couple clients periodically dangle the fat-paycheck, paid-benefits carrot under my nose—usually when I'm having a slow quarter and dipping into my emergency fund to pay my bills. Most of the time I tell them, "Thanks, but no thanks." Every once in a while, though, I raise an eyebrow and say, "I'm listening . . ." Sometimes I even make it as far as the interview.

The point is, when it comes to finding work that makes your entrepreneurial heart go pitter-pat, there is no "Easy" button, no silver bullet, no over-the-counter boss-loss pill you can take. There's you and your enterprising resourcefulness and your persistent, if not stubborn, desire to make this crazy way we have of spending most of our waking hours more bearable, or even, dare I say, enjoyable. I've given you the tools you need to get going, the main course at this career potluck, if you will. Now it's up to you to bring the necessary appetite and utensils to the table.

After all, there's more to life than working for some boss who barks out orders like a drill sergeant but can't even reach the fax machine himself.

NO-FEAR Negotiation

Whether you work in an office, in a laboratory, or outside on a job site, knowing how to negotiate salary (and a raise) is a must. Maybe today you're a union gal, or beholden to a fixed hourly rate based on seniority. But you never know where you might find yourself down the line. And just like a killer resume, no-fear negotiation is a tool that can help your career enormously, no matter what industry you work in.

Before you can negotiate confidently, you have to assess your market value based on geography, skill level, and experience. "A lot of people stay in denial," says Sherri Edwards of Resource Maximizer, a pull-no-punches career-coaching firm. For the most accurate going rate, don't stop at the Salary.com stats. If you live in, say, Boston, the wages you're pulling up online may be averages of metropolitan salaries of those in the burbs or boonies. To further investigate, poll the pros in your field with questions like, "So, what could someone in this region at my skill level expect to earn?" (Notice how I didn't say to ask others what *they* earn, which would be rude.)

Before you reach the negotiation table, Edwards recommends writing up a list of your tangible career accomplishments—successes that have benefited your *employers.* Maybe you implemented a department-wide training program that raised productivity by 25 percent, or created the first intelligible manual for using your team's customized software. You get the idea.

When it comes time to talk dollars, try to get the hiring manager to cough up their preferred salary range first. Either way, point to your achievements and the going price for someone with your cachet before you say, "This is the range I'm comfortable with." Do give the hiring manager a salary range you'd like, not just a flat figure. You need to give yourself a cushion. That way, if they negotiate down your salary, you still wind up with a wage you can live with. For example, say your research shows that a person with your experience can command a $45,000 annual salary in your city, and you decide you won't take the job for anything less than $43,000. So you tell the hiring manager you're comfortable with a salary range of $45,000 to $50,000, giving yourself some wiggle room should the hiring manager haggle.

Finally, don't beg, whine, argue, or quibble over trivial amounts. It's unbecoming. If the company can't meet your dollar amount, see if you can negotiate an extra week's vacation or paid tuition for that computer-programming class you've been meaning to take.

Know that if you're the new kid on the block, you won't have much bargaining power. In other words, if the entry-level salary for a gig you're interested in is in the $30,000 to $35,000 range, you won't be able to ask for $45,000—unless maybe you're a child prodigy.

These suggestions apply to temp and flex jobs, too. But for haggling with potential clients when you're self-employed, see Chapter 6. When you're the boss, the game is played a little differently.

a TEMP'S Survival Guide

Whether you're on assignment for two weeks or ten months, temping is a gig unto itself. At its worst, you could feel like the corporate orphans in the movie *Clockwatchers,* subject to such workplace indignities as being corralled into a "temp station" in the middle of the office, denied adequate office supplies, or renamed "Hey you." At its best, you could feel like graphic novelist Sara Varon, who emailed me giddy over her "really, really fun" temp gig working for the Golden Gloves amateur boxing competition in New York City, a job that entailed attending four months of boxing matches.

Most likely, your experiences as a temp will fall somewhere in between—nothing as melodramatic as being escorted out on your ass by security for stealing one pen too many, and nothing quite as thrilling as a Madison Square Garden boxing match. Either way, temping gives you a window into another world you may not have seen otherwise. And whether you're a bricklayer or a web builder, there are some things you can do to make sure your stint as a temp is as painless—hell, even as enjoyable—as possible.

A TEMPING PRIMER

If you've never contemplated the pros and cons of temping or contracting, allow me to give you the lowdown. As I said earlier in the book, temping is a nice option for worker bees looking to infiltrate their dream field, people who want a paycheck but not a traditional j-o-b, and newbie freelancers looking to supplement a spotty workload. In fact, thanks to companies looking to cut costs, temping is on the rise: In the first quarter of 2006, the American Staffing Association (ASA) reported that U.S. staffing firms placed about 2.9 million temps a day—up 5.5 percent from the first quarter of 2005. And a 2006 U.S. Chamber of Commerce report says 4 percent of all workers are contingent staff (basically permatemps).

Yes, temp agencies pay a lower hourly rate than you can earn working for yourself, but they have the contacts to keep you busy month after month, and they pay you every two weeks like clockwork (unlike freelance clients). The ASA says the average temp makes at least $12 an hour, though I know many seasoned writer, editor, producer, designer, and programmer temps around the country who make two to four times that, some with overtime to boot. It depends on your industry, skills, experience level, and geographic location. And while the ASA says most temp agencies offer health, retirement, and vacation benefits, I've always found the temp bennies I'm offered—that is, if I'm offered them—greatly pared down from what my employee pals get. Then again, it's more benefits than I'd have as a freelancer.

If not having a staff job makes you uneasy, I won't sugarcoat it: Temping may be a tough road for you. For one thing, it's incredibly easy for the company you're working at to cut you loose at a moment's notice, given that they have no legal obligation to keep you around. For another thing, it's incredibly easy for said company to keep you on the permatemp carousel for months or years on end, even if you pine for a permanent position.

Depending on whom you ask, temps (or contract workers) move on to permanent work anywhere from 5 to 75 percent of the time. That's why Cynthia Shapiro, author of *Corporate Confidential: 50 Secrets Your Company Doesn't Want You to Know—And What to Do About Them,* advises that you examine the track record of the company you're temping at: "Do they ever hire temps as perms, or do they just keep them in the corner?" When you're gunning for a steady staff gig, the company that pigeonholes its temps for years on end isn't such a good bet.

YOU AND YOUR AGENCY

The United States is home to thousands of temp agencies. Before you get in bed with one of them, sniff them out just as you would any other employer. To find the best agencies, ask the locals in your field for recommendations. Also see what advice you can glean from worker-advocacy groups, like WashTech.org and online communities like the New York–centric Red Guide to Temp Agencies (www.redguide.grieve-smith.com).

When you meet with the agency for the first time, you may have to take a bunch of tests to prove that you can use a computer without causing smoke to billow out of it. Or you may have to show off samples of your work. All this will depend on the gig you're applying for and the field you're in. For longer-term contracts, you may also have to interview with the company you'll be working at.

If I could offer only four words of advice about working with contract-placement agencies, they'd be: *Negotiate your ass off.* (If you need a refresher, see the "No-Fear Negotiation" section of the appendix.) Temp agencies bill the "client" (the company you work at) far more than you get paid, often marking up your hourly rate by 20, 50, even 100 percent. For that reason, there's often some wiggle room on the hourly rate you can get. Be realistic about your experience level; if you're new to the industry, you may have to take a lower rate to sneak through the door.

If the agency's falling all over itself trying to get you on its payroll but not meeting your rate, don't be afraid to ask for a more flex work situation—what Ellen Parker, a former recruiter at a West Coast staffing agency, calls "a new kind of compensation"—from alternative hours to partial telecommuting. I know I'm spoiled, but I won't even consider a temp gig anymore if it doesn't involve some telecommuting.

Get on the radar of more than one agency to boost your chances for landing a plum assignment. Have patience, and periodically check in with your agency reps by phone or email to remind them you're ready, willing, and able to work. Agencies deal with truckloads of temps a year, so they appreciate these polite pings. However, they don't appreciate daily stalkers, so consider yourself warned. And if the agency tells you to gussy up your resume so you're more marketable to their clients, do so. Otherwise, you have no business complaining about their dogging you.

Speaking of resumes, as a person who hops from temp gig to temp gig, your CV will look a bit different than it did when you had a staff job—mainly because you'll have more gigs to list now. Ask a couple of successful temps to show you their resume so you can see how they've formatted it, or see if they've posted it to their website. The Contract Employee's Handbook (www.cehandbook.com) is another good resource for resume tips.

Finally, read your temp agency's contract carefully. If you can't understand a lick of it, ask a savvy temp pal or your lawyer friend to decipher it. Or consult an industry organization like the National Writers Union or Graphic Artists Guild. Be on the lookout for a "non-compete clause" in your agency contract, the clause that says you won't steal your agency's contacts if you go into business for yourself. Although it's perfectly understandable the agency wouldn't want you to pilfer their clients, if you hope to freelance directly for the company you're assigned to someday, you may want to renegotiate (or rethink) the contract.

YOU AND YOUR ASSIGNMENT

On your first day as a temp, cliché-happy managers will say they expect you to be a "self-starter" who can "hit the ground running" because "it's sink or swim around here." Don't let this freak you out. Basically, this is code for, "We don't have the time, money, or inclination to train you, so if you want to still be here in a week, we suggest you learn the ropes yourself." Sure, they'll show you the basics, like where you should sit and where the bathroom is. But it will be up to you to fill in many of the blanks—essentially, to train yourself. The only way to do this is to ask a ton of questions, and not necessarily of your manager, whom you may find has an uncanny knack for being about as helpful as a broken copy machine.

That said, with the right mindset, you can handle even the most harrowing temp assignment. Following are my top tips culled from years working in the ranks of this country's career nomads.

Find full-time allies. Some full-time employees (a.k.a. FTEs) will treat you like temp trash; others will treat you like their next of kin. Find your FTE allies early on. Take everyone you can to coffee and ask how you'll be working with them. Often, you'll get the inside scoop on the team politics (e.g., why your department's the black sheep of the company) and insights that can save you time in your daily work (e.g., where you can download the software you need to do the job they hired you to do). If your newfound FTE pals want to vent about their coworkers, don't chime in—it can come back to haunt you. Instead, just smile and nod.

Be the queen of flex. Go With The Flow is every temp's middle name. If your manager has been hitting the caffeine too hard, she may ask you to change gears on that Very Important Project you're doing no less than five times before Tuesday. Practice your poker face—you'll need it often. Never voice your disdain aloud, unless you have a very, very constructive suggestion. Accept the fact that you're now responsible for all projects no one else has the time or inclination to do. As a temp, picking up the trash is your job description.

Manage your manager. Going with the flow is one thing. Rolling over like a puppy piddling herself is another. If your manager's prone to dumping rush projects on your desk at 4:59 PM, stage a preemptive strike. Tell her after lunch that you have a five-thirty doctor's appointment and can't stay a minute after five, so if she has any rush work she wants done today, you'll need to get started on it ASAP. And if your manager's MIA whenever you need her to sign off on something (like your timecard), ambush her. Send emails, voice mails, interoffice memos, smoke signals—whatever it takes to get her attention.

When in Rome . . . The line between FTEs and temps is often nebulous. Sometimes you'll find yourself faking your way through a meeting about an upcoming project that you won't be around long enough to work on. (Remember, poker face.) Maybe you'll be asked for your input, maybe you won't. Maybe you'll speak up and everyone will look at you like there's a horn growing out of your forehead. If you're not sure where your role begins and ends, ask your manager, your temp agency, or your fellow transients.

Befriend your fellow temps. Believe me, you'll need the support. Bitch about your job if you must, but know that excessive boss-trashing is the quickest route to developing a chip on your shoulder the size of California. It's more uplifting to bond over your lives outside the temp corral. My last temp family and I held karaoke lunches on Fridays. Two cubemates brought in their guitars and basically led the rest of us in '80s-pop sing-alongs. Goofy stuff like this just makes the job more human.

Don't wait till your last day to schmooze. Start scouting out your next temp gig before your current one ends. Some temp agencies and companies discourage temps from "networking" on the job. Fine, so don't blanket the office with unsolicited copies of your resume (a tacky move anyway). But if you like working with your FTE allies and would be happy to do so again sometime, tell them as much. Tell your temp agency too. Managers and agencies live for temps who already know how to do the job. In fact, I've had a number of requests to reprise my past temp gigs and to interview for staff jobs in departments I've temped for.

"Temp" is not a four-letter word. Be proud that you're indie and not shackled by the golden handcuffs. True, you may not get invited to the company picnic (hell, I've witnessed FTE-only happy hours in the hallway right outside my office). But you can't let that eat at you—after all, you're not a company employee. Instead, you're the one who gets to leave after eight hours without worrying about whether you've put in enough overtime to warrant a promotion. You're the one who's devoting extra time to your artwork or starting a new business on the side. The beauty of this gig is that it's only temporary.

Boss in a BOX

*S*ome critical pieces of running your own business may not come naturally to you—things like taxes, business law, and figuring out why the computer's making that bloodcurdling noise, for instance. Since you can't run a business if you can't make sense of your contracts or your computer blows up, hiring (or bartering with) an accountant, lawyer, or computer whiz who knows the score is well worth the cost.

Regardless of whether you call in the big guns or master all the nuances of self-employment yourself, there are a few logistics you should know. This section will get you started.

HOW TO GET LEGIT

Hanging your shingle entails a bit more than nailing a sign that reads THE DOCTOR IS IN to a makeshift advice booth, like Lucy of Peanuts fame did. Take the time to get legit from the get-go. The last thing you need is some government office breathing down your neck in the middle of your crunch to fill all your summer orders for same-sex wedding-cake toppers. Some of the essentials of setting up shop follow. (If, after doing the research, any of these seem like overkill for your particular industry or workload—say, if you're just illustrating a couple newspaper articles a month on the side and barely making a profit—you may want to skip them for now.)

Is this name taken? Name your baby as soon as possible. Your domain name, website, business cards, and letterhead depend on it.

So do any business licenses, permits, and legal documentation you need. Pick a name you love enough to tattoo on your arm, because you'll (hopefully) be stuck with it for years to come. Before you commit, poll friends and family to see if it's catchy and clearly conveys your MO. Do a city, state, and national search to make sure someone isn't already using your name. (To learn how, see the next section.)

Licensed to sell. Depending on where you live, you may need a city or state business license, or both. Same goes for permits, especially if you're feeding people, getting them drunk, watching their kids, or otherwise serving the public. Your local chamber of commerce, county clerk's office, or state department of licensing can clue you in to regional license and permit requirements (a web search on "[your state here] business license" is a good place to start). License requirements and fees also vary from vocation to vocation, so a plumber won't necessarily have the same requirements as a technical editor.

Register as a woman-owned business. If you're hoping to land government or Fortune 500 contracts, registering as a woman-owned business has the potential to boost your sales and help you better compete against the big guns in your industry. Reason being, governments and corporations often have internal policies on giving preference to woman- and minority-owned businesses.

For $300 to $350, you can register as a women-owned business with the Women's Business Enterprise National Council (WBENC). Know that the application process is time-consuming and the turnaround is slow. Check the WBENC site (www.wbenc.org) for details. As an alternative, you can register with your state's women and minority business office. Before you decide where to register, check with your potential customers to see which certification they recognize.

Bells and whistles. A few business services and supplies are worth investing in: a business checking account to keep your personal and professional stashes separate. A dedicated business line or cell phone. Easy-to-learn bookkeeping software (I use Excel; many business owners I know prefer an accounting program like QuickBooks). Membership in a professional organization or two. Depending on the type of business you're in, you may also need business accoutre-ments like merchant credit card status, a toll-free number, or a mes-senger service. As long as they're elemental to running your business, these services are tax write-offs.

Cover your ass. You'd be wise to get business liability insurance so if a customer slips on a banana peel in your clown-supply store, you don't lose the (balloon-covered) shirt off your back. Take the time to read up on the different types of business insurance. About.com is a good place to start. Some cash-cow clients may require you to have certain professional insurance policies before they will work with you, such as errors and omissions (E&O) insurance, which protects your hide if, say, the brochure you designed for a Montessori school gets printed with a four-letter word in it. I know that throughout this book I've spouted off on the merits of starting as simply and inex-pensively as you can. But it only takes one nasty lawsuit to put you out of business and back in the cube from whence you came.

To lease or not to lease? Explore all available options before you commit to a traditional lease, especially if your business doesn't require brick-and-mortar digs. Consider selling your macramé handbags through the web, a cheaply rented artist's studio, or your favorite beauty salon or vintage shop, rather than opening your own storefront. Some business incubators, like the one offered by the Renaissance Entrepreneurship Center in San Francisco, offer month-to-month office space and professional services you can rent for less than the going rate. Regardless of whom you rent from, Sha-ron Miller, CEO of the Renaissance Entrepreneurship Center, rec-ommends having six months' commercial rent and utilities saved up before you sign a lease.

A word to the wise: *If working from your own abode or garage, check that your city and county zoning laws don't ban home-based businesses.* Some do. (Whether they enforce this ban is another story, but who wants to risk having their handcrafted furniture empire run out of town?) Do this *before* you apply for that business license so you don't get nailed.

ALPHABET SOUP: HOW TO MAKE
SENSE OF THE LEGALESE

What's behind the alphabet soup of solo work? Websites like Nolo.com, LegalZoom.com, and Lawyers.com kindly translate all the legal mumbo jumbo into plain English. To get you started, here's a cheat sheet.

Doing business as (DBA). To use a business name other than your own, you need to file a DBA—a.k.a. a fictitious business name—with your county government. Contact your county clerk's office to do this *before* you apply for your business license, print up business cards, and do all that other legwork (in case someone's already using the name you want). You can even do this online through websites like MyCorporation.com.

Independent contractor (IC). If no one's the boss of you (you work solo for various clients, rather than as an employee), the IRS considers you an independent contractor. Freelancers, consultants, and free agents are ICs. Clients legally can tell you what projects they want done, but you call the shots on when, where, and how you'll get the job done. Since ICs are self-employed, they pay their own benefits.

Sole proprietor. If you work independently as a book indexer, baby photographer, or belly-dancing instructor, you are automatically a sole proprietor. According to the IRS website (www.irs.gov), this is the "simplest form of business organization to start and maintain," and "its liabilities are your personal liabilities." In other words, if someone stiffs, sues, or otherwise bleeds your business dry, they stiff, sue, or otherwise bleed *you* dry.

Partnership. Just like it sounds, a partnership is a business owned by more than one person. Partners share in the expenses, workload, and profits (or losses). To transfer the personal liability of business ownership to the company, partners can file papers with their state to become a corporation or a limited liability company (LLC).

Corporation. Small-business owners sometimes go the corporation route, or "get incorporated," to protect their personal assets (the

$100 in your piggy bank or the home you scrimped and saved for) from the debts and monetary mishaps of their business. Doing so entails paying a bunch of fees and filing a ream of paperwork with your state. Besides protecting yourself from losing everything you own if your business tanks, forming a corporation can land you big-fish clients that don't normally work with sole proprietors.

Limited liability company (LLC). In a way, LLCs are a happy medium between sole proprietorships and full-blown corporations. Like a corporation, you are protected against the financial foul-ups and hardships of your business. An LLC requires some legal paperwork to set up, which will cost you a small chunk of change, and is governed by a bunch of government rules and regs. But it's easier and cheaper to set up and operate than a corporation.

Franchise. Ben & Jerry's and Mrs. Fields are franchises. Opening a franchise—becoming a "franchisee"—means licensing the business name and model from an established enterprise. In exchange for the start-up fee and sales percentage you pay the parent company, you get a proven, bank loan–friendly business plan and built-in business assistance from the mother ship (your franchise's HQ). The downside is, you have to wear the goofy uniforms they want you to, decorate the place the way they say, and adhere to their business guidelines. *Entrepreneur* magazine rates the top 500 franchises, best home-based franchises, and least costly franchises at Entrepreneur .com/franzone.

Nonprofit corporation. According to Nolo.com, "A nonprofit corporation is a corporation formed to carry out a charitable, educational, religious, literary, or scientific purpose." Nonprofits don't pay federal or state income taxes on the money they make, provided said profits stem from activities related to the organization's mission. Some people refer to nonprofits as 501(c)(3) corporations because that's the part of the federal tax code that most commonly applies to them.

HOW TO PAY YOUR TAXES

As I've already implied, paying taxes as a business owner is way more complicated than doing so as a standard employee. Because you are the employer *and* employee now, you send your taxes directly to the IRS, as well as your city and state, local laws depending. You also pay both the "employer" half of your social security and Medicare taxes (which your 9-to-5 job kindly covered for you) and the "employee" half. And you'll need to save all your receipts for those golden tax write-offs.

Find out from the get-go how your business is required to pay city, state, and federal taxes. It will vary widely, depending on whether you're legally classified as a solo proprietor, an LLC, a partnership, a franchise, or a corporation with employees. For example, if you work solo as a carpenter, caretaker, or candlestick maker, Uncle Sam will want you to pay taxes quarterly, which may sound ugly but is far less painful than the prospect of paying in one lump sum each year.

You'll find much of this information on your city and state licensing websites, and on IRS.gov. But all this tax business is made far simpler (and less migraine inducing) if you find a good accountant in your state to prepare your tax returns and help decipher anything you don't understand. I've also asked my accountant to show me how to do some of the easier sole-proprietor stuff, like filing my annual city and state tax returns so I don't have to rely on him for everything. That said, tax laws change every year. Knowing exactly how is not at the top of my to-do list—another reason why it pays to work with an accountant.

Must-See
RESOURCES

consulted many, many books, websites, and other resources while writing this book, many of them recommended to me by the smart and insightful women I talked to. The following are among my favorites.

Get your money straight

The Money Book for the Young, Fabulous & Broke, by Suze Orman, Riverhead Books, 2005. Yeah, I resisted checking out what Suze had to say for years, too. But the woman makes sense. More important, she makes managing your money (or lack thereof) easy to understand.

My Misspent Youth, by Meghan Daum, Open City Books, 2001. If this collection's title essay (also found at www.meghandaum.com) doesn't convince you to downsize your lifestyle and stop living beyond your means, I don't know what will.

www.moneymanagement.org. Got credit card debt? Consumer Credit Counseling Service can help knock down your interest payments and shave years off your debt repayment. Be prepared to cut up your cards; you won't find any sympathy for your shoe addiction here.

Salary sites like www.salary.com, www.salaryexpert.com, and the U.S. Bureau of Labor Statistics' National Compensation Survey (www.bls .gov/ncs) should be one of your first stops when contemplating a new career path.

What color is your nose ring?

I Don't Know What I Want, But I Know It's Not This: A Step-by-Step Guide to Finding Gratifying Work, by Julie Jansen, Penguin Books, 2003. An excellent guide for those stumped about where they want work to take them next. Loaded with helpful quizzes and not a trace of woo-woo.

What Should I Do with My Life? The True Story of People Who Answered the Ultimate Question, by Po Bronson, Random House, 2002. You won't find any ten step plans here. Instead, you'll find a gorgeously written account of how several dozen very real people—women, men, young, old, well off, struggling—have chosen to answer the timeless question.

www.careerjournal.com. Don't let the fact that this is a *Wall Street Journal* site scare you away. The site's exploding with endlessly helpful articles on everything from revamping your resume and negotiating pay to changing career paths and working abroad. Yes, the examples in the articles are usually vanilla execs who live in the burbs, but that doesn't mean you can't take the free tips and run.

Razzle-dazzle 'em

Resume Magic: Trade Secrets of a Professional Resume Writer, Second Edition and *Interview Magic: Job Interview Secrets from America's Career and Life Coach,* by Susan Britton Whitcomb, JIST Works, 2003 and 2004, respectively. The titles pretty much say it all.

www.collegegrad.com. Endlessly helpful interview, resume, and cover-letter tips for workforce newbies. Don't miss the exhaustive list of free resume templates.

Small-Talk Savvy: Operator's Manual, by Melissa Wadsworth, Adams Media Corporation, 2005 (available through www.bordersstores.com). Down-to-earth tips on how to not look, feel, and act like a dork when meeting new people in your dream profession.

A little action on the side (a.k.a. "So, how's that book coming along?")

Bird by Bird: Some Instructions on Writing and Life, by Anne Lamott, Pantheon, 1994. Not just for writers, this is a great read for anyone with a project they can't seem to get off the ground. Anne Lamott knows how to rally the troops. At the very least, she'll make you laugh yourself silly.

The Creative Habit: Learn It and Use It for Life, by Twyla Tharp, Simon & Schuster, 2003. This choreography legend takes the mystery out of building a creative routine and offers a number of exercises to help you get there. No need to slog through *The Artist's Way.* All you need to know is here.

The Procrastinator's Handbook: Mastering the Art of Doing It Now, by Rita Emmett, Walker, 2000. Another gem for those whose novel, camera, or business plan has accumulated a thick film of dust. I originally read this immensely helpful little book while procrastinating. Fortunately, it was a quick read. Even better, it taught me how to stop stalling.

Flex your schedule

Going Part Time: The Insider's Guide for Professional Women Who Want a Career and a Life, by Cindy Tolliver and Nancy Chambers, Avon Books, 1997. Even though this book is a little older, it's loaded with great information about the pros and cons of flex work, as well as how to broach the subject with the boss and write a killer proposal.

www.workoptions.com. Brimming with tips on nabbing that elusive work/life balance, and nominally priced templates (I'm talking under $20 or $30) you can use to jump-start your own flex-work proposal.

The 100 Best Companies to Work For list. According to *Working Mother* magazine (www.workingmother.com/100BEST_2005.html) and *Fortune* magazine (www.money.cnn.com/magazines/fortune/best companies), these are good places to find life-friendly employers.

Know that the cute little mom-and-pop bike shop down the road from you won't be on their radar.

www.cehandbook.com. The Contract Employee's Handbook, much of which can be read online. Required reading for anyone thinking about working on a several-month contract with a staffing or temporary agency. Don't miss the resume tips for permatemps.

www.momsrising.org. Schmooze and organize with other working mothers, courtesy of Joan Blades and Kristin Rowe-Finkbeiner, authors of *The Motherhood Manifesto: What America's Moms Want—And What to Do About It*. Portions of the book are posted on the site.

You're the boss

www.score.org. If you're thinking of self-employment, SCORE, Counselors to America's Small Business, should be your first stop. This nonprofit offers a gold mine of start-up information, training, and free counseling. Check out the resources aimed at women and minorities, as well as the templates for business plans and other essentials.

A Girl's Guide to Starting Your Own Business: Candid Advice, Frank Talk, and True Stories for the Successful Entrepreneur, by Caitlin Friedman and Kimberly Yorio. Once you get past the pink cover font, you'll find a treasure trove of start-up information inside.

What to Charge: Pricing Strategies for Freelancers and Consultants, by Laurie Lewis, Aletheia Publications, 2000. An invaluable guide.

www.microenterpriseworks.org. See the site's Resources page to find a microlending organization in your neck of the woods for entrepreneurial training, advice, and/or microloans (loans up to $35,000).

www.count-me-in.org. The first online microlending program (loans of $500 to $10,000) for women business owners. Endorsed by the National Association of Women Business Owners.

217

www.nbia.org. See the site's Resource Center to find a business incubator near you to help grow your venture and provide affordable office space and professional services.

The do-gooder's guide to the galaxy

Grassroots: A Field Guide for Feminist Activism, by Jennifer Baumgardner and Amy Richards, Farrar, Straus and Giroux, 2004. Whether you want to hold a house party or start a grassroots organization, this book will give you more than enough ideas and inspiration to make it happen.

Making the News: A Guide for Activists and Nonprofits, by Jason Salzman, Perseus Books, 2003. Publicity and PR made plain and simple. Not just for activists and nonprofit founders.

www.idealist.org. A clearinghouse for all things nonprofit. Paid and volunteer job listings, job fair announcements, frequently asked questions, resources for nonprofit founders, and more.

Nonprofit job sites galore: See www.volunteermatch.org if you're looking for a volunteer gig; www.boardnetusa.org if you're looking for a board in search of members; and www.opportunityknocks.org if you're looking for a paid gig.

www.compasspoint.org/askgenie. The ultimate FAQ resource for nonprofit founders, board members, and volunteers.

www.foundationcenter.org. The Foundation Center site is packed with information about grant and other philanthropic programs. A must for anyone looking to seriously fundraise.

Legal aid

www.nolo.com. The best friend in law you ever had. Translates self-employment law, business start-up basics, nonprofit law and fundraising, copyright issues, contracts, and incorporation into plain English. Don't miss the countless Nolo books available on many of these topics, too.

Tech support

www.geeksquad.com. Your very own help desk for hire. For those who hate to read the manual, or who can't for the life of them figure out why their computer's crashing every time they turn it on. If you don't have any techie friends, Geek Squad—open 24/7—is your new BFF.

www.techsoup.org. Free and low-cost tech info and support for non-profits. Don't miss TechSoup Stock, where "nonprofits can access donated and discounted technology products, generously provided by corporate and nonprofit technology partners."

Insure thine ass

www.ahirc.org. Access to Health Insurance/Resources for Care, a comprehensive guide to health insurance options, by state. For additional health insurance options for the self-employed, check out professional organizations such as Media Bistro (national: www.mediabistro.com); Freelancers Union (New York: www.freelancersunion.org); or Media Alliance (Oakland, California: www.media-alliance.org).

Road maps for expats

Adventure Divas: Searching the Globe for a New Kind of Heroine, by Holly Morris, Villard, 2005, and www.adventuredivas.com. Read the book for inspiration to go anywhere you set your mind to and the website for tips on how to get there.

Delaying the Real World: A Twentysomething's Guide to Seeking Adventure, by Colleen Kinder, Running Press, 2005. This book nearly had me out the door and on the next plane. If you're looking for ideas for volunteer and paid travel gigs, run to the nearest bookstore or library and pick this baby up.

The Back Door Guide to Short Term Adventures, Fourth Edition, by Michael Landes, Ten Speed Press, 2005. Same as above. The jam-packed reference (more than 1,000 U.S. and international gigs listed) will have you wondering why you've been working at a desk for the past umpteen months. Also see the website: www.backdoorjobs.com.

www.transitionsabroad.com. Loaded with resources for anyone who wants to work, volunteer, study, travel, or move abroad.

For classic off-the-beaten path travel guides, see Lonely Planet (www.lonelyplanet.com) and Moon Handbooks (www.moon.com).

Women in hard hats, Carhartts, or uniforms

300 Best Jobs Without a Four-Year Degree, by Michael Farr and LaVerne L. Ludden, JIST Works, 2002. Using U.S. Department of Labor stats, the authors aggregate hundreds of job categories and rate them based on earnings, projected growth rate, and annual job openings. There's even a section on part-time and self-employed career opportunities. Cool.

Hard-Hatted Women: Stories of Struggle and Success in the Trades, edited by Molly Martin, Seal Press, 1988. If you're thinking of boldly going where most women have not gone before, these tales of women who work in male-dominated fields will inspire you.

www.tradeswomennow.org. Tradeswomen Now and Tomorrow is a "national coalition of tradeswomen's organizations and advocates." Check out their member page to find an organization supporting women in the trades or offering an apprenticeship program near you.

No woman working in an ultra-male field should go without support. To get yourself a piece of the sisterhood, check out organizations like National Association of Women in Construction (www.nawic.org), Women in the Fire Service (www.wfsi.org), and The Ninety-Nines, International Organization of Women Pilots (www.ninety-nines.org).

Know your rights

Don't go into the workforce blind. Get to know the rules and regs proscribed by the government, as well as the pressing issues for women today. If you need information or advocacy, these resources can help: 9to5, National Association for Working Women (www.9to5 .org), National Women's Law Center (www.nwlc.org), and the U.S. Equal Employment Opportunity Commission (www.eeoc.gov).

the RAMBLING
Academy Awards Speech

There are a few people I'd like to thank. Without them, I never would have finished this book, let alone started the dang thing.

Debbie Stoller at *Bust*, Andi Zeisler at *Bitch*, and Anne Hurley and Carey Gelernter at *The Seattle Times* for giving me a venue to write about women who work outside the cube. Undying gratitude. Truly.

My ultra-supportive editors at Seal. This wild ride started with Brooke Warner, who egged me on, egged me on some more, then signed me up. And paging Jill Rothenberg: You are a true rock star. Thank you so much for shepherding me and my manuscript through. This peppermint ice cream cone's for you. Also, a big shout-out to my other Seal heroes: Laura Mazer, Annie Tucker, Darcy Cohan, and Leslie Royal. Rock stars, all.

The generous folks who made my stay at Hedgebrook the stuff writer dreams are made of, and the talented other women with whom I shared my time there—Alia, Amy, Beena, Marian, Sunny, and Traci—I'm forever yours in chocolate solidarity.

The many friends and pros who lent their eyes and ears along the way, most notably Greg Beckelhymer, Sheila Bender, Bill Ehardt, Angela Jane Fountas, John Gile, Alle Hall, Traci Macnamara, Diane Mapes, Sarah McCormic, Marcia Paul, Renate Raymond, Ariel Meadow Stallings, and Lisa Wogan. "Thanks a mil" hardly begins to cover it.

The umpteen career, business, and financial experts who shared their razor-sharp insights with me: Jill Badonsky, Jennifer Baumgardner, Melody Biringer, Janet Boguch, Cindia Cameron, Kristy Carter, Gwynn Cassidy, Sherri Edwards, Lynn Gagliardi, Anastasia

Goodstein, Kristen Grimm, Alice Hanson, Julie Jansen, Kirsten Johnson, Anya Kamenetz, Colleen Kinder, Lisa Kivirist, Elaine Lee, Lynn Shiori Miyauchi, Gail McMeekin, Sharon Miller, Holly Morris, Susan Murphy, Amy Richards, Alexandra Robbins, Curt Rosengren, Kristin Rowe-Finkbeiner, Janet Scarborough, Beth Schoenfeldt, Cynthia Shapiro, Keri Smith, Barbara Stanny, Melissa Wadsworth, and Debbie Webber.

The clients, temp agencies, and part-time bosses I've worked with over the years who have kept a roof over my head (and given me so much great fodder)—thanks. The "Me Too" Crew in Ballard, for their tireless cheerleading. My parents, for accepting early on that I was never going to "get a real job." Naomi, for always rallying behind me and getting it. Greg, for giving me the room to go off in my corner, and for being there no matter how insane (or unkempt) I got. You are the best.

Of course, this book would not have been possible without all the cubicle expats who so generously shared their anti 9-to-5 stories and suggestions with me. To all you fearless women, I am endlessly grateful.

ABOUT THE AUTHOR

Michelle Goodman escaped from the cube in 1992 and has been a freelance writer and editor ever since (with the occasional temp gig thrown in for good measure). To keep a roof over her head, she wrangles print and online text for high-tech empires, book publishers, and peddlers of new age philosophy. Her articles about alternative careers, human mating rituals, and pop culture have appeared in *Bust, Bitch, The Bark, The Seattle Times, Salon,* and the anthology *The Moment of Truth: Women's Funniest Romantic Catastrophes.* She lives in Seattle with her eighty-pound lapdog, Buddy. Visit her blog at www.anti9to5guide.com.

© photo credit Greg Beckelhymer

SELECTED TITLES FROM SEAL PRESS

For more than thirty years, Seal Press has published groundbreaking books. By women. For women. Visit our website at www.sealpress.com.

What Would Murphy Brown Do? How the Women of Prime Time Changed Our Lives by Allison Klein. $15.95, 1-58005-171-5. From workplace politics to single motherhood to designer heels in the city, revisit TV's favorite—and most influential—women of the 1970s through today.

Indecent: How I Make It and Fake It as a Girl for Hire by Sarah Katherine Lewis. $14.95, 1-58005-169-3. An insider reveals the gritty reality behind the alluring facade of the sex industry.

Women in Overdrive: Find Balance and Overcome Burnout at Any Age by Nora Isaacs. $14.95, 1-58005-161-8. For women who take on more than they can handle, this book highlights how women of different age sets are affected by overdrive and what they can do to avoid burnout.

She's Such a Geek: Women Write About Science, Technology, and Other Nerdy Stuff edited by Annalee Newitz and Charlie Anders. $14.95, 1-58005-190-1. From comic books and gaming to science fiction and blogging, nerdy women have their say in this witty collection that takes on the "boys only" clubs and celebrates a woman's geek spirit.

Stalking the Wild Dik-Dik: One Woman's Solo Misadventures Across Africa by Marie Javins. $15.95, 1-58005-164-2. A funny and compassionate account of the sort of lively and heedless undertaking that could only happen in Africa.

Job Hopper: The Checkered Career of a Down-Market Dilettante by Ayun Halliday. $14.95, 1-58005-130-8. Halliday, quickly becoming one of America's funniest writers, chronicles her hilarious misadventures in the working world.